The Financial Times Guide to
Executive Health

FT Prentice Hall

FINANCIAL TIMES

In an increasingly competitive world, we believe it's quality of thinking that will give you the edge – an idea that opens new doors, a technique that solves a problem, or an insight that simply makes sense of it all. The more you know, the smarter and faster you can go.

That's why we work with the best minds in business and finance to bring cutting-edge thinking and best learning practice to a global market.

Under a range of leading imprints, including Financial Times Prentice Hall, we create world-class print publications and electronic products bringing our readers knowledge, skills and understanding which can be applied whether studying or at work.

To find out more about our business publications, or tell us about the books you'd like to find, you can visit us at
www.business-minds.com

For other Pearson Education publications, visit
www.pearsoned-ema.com

The Financial Times Guide to
Executive Health

Building your strengths, managing your risks

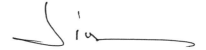

To Michael –
With great appreciation for help in
freeing the FDL with which we were
able to move the work forward.
... and Portuguese, Greek, Russian,
Thai, and ??? international editions are
a nice bonus.

James Campbell Quick, Cary L. Cooper,
Jonathan D. Quick MD and Joanne H. Gavin

Low and hard, front sight comer –

Jim

FT Prentice Hall
FINANCIAL TIMES

London ● New York ● San Francisco ● Toronto ● Sydney ● Tokyo ● Singapore
Hong Kong ● Cape Town ● Madrid ● Paris ● Milan ● Munich ● Amsterdam

PEARSON EDUCATION LIMITED

Head Office:
Edinburgh Gate
Harlow CM20 2JE
Tel: +44 (0)1279 623623
Fax: +44 (0)1279 431059

London Office:
128 Long Acre
London WC2E 9AN
Tel: +44 (0)20 7447 2000
Fax: +44 (0)20 7447 2170
Website: www.business-minds.com

First published in Great Britain in 2002

© Pearson Education Limited 2002

The rights of James Campbell Quick, Cary L. Cooper, Jonathan D. Quick and
Joanne H. Gavin to be identified as Authors of this work have been asserted by
them in accordance with the Copyright, Designs and Patents Act 1988.

ISBN 0 273 65428 4

British Library Cataloguing in Publication Data
A CIP catalogue record for this book can be obtained from the British Library.

10 9 8 7 6 5 4 3 2 1

Designed by designdeluxe
Typeset by Northern Phototypesetting Co. Ltd, Bolton
Printed and bound in Great Britain by Biddles Ltd, Guildford & King's Lynn

The Publishers' policy is to use paper manufactured from sustainable forests.

Contents

Acknowledgments

The authors express their appreciation to Rachael Stock, their editor at the *Financial Times* in London, for her support and encouragement in the development of this book. The authors would like to acknowledge three sources of support for the research that serves as the foundation for this work. First, BUPA, the largest medical insurance company and private hospital group in the United Kingdom, has substantially funded Cary L. Cooper's research group at University of Manchester Institute of Science & Technology (UMIST). Second, James Campbell Quick in the Center for Research on Organizational and Managerial Excellence at the University of Texas at Arlington and Jonathan D. Quick at the World Health Organization appreciate a trust gift given to support their program of research in executive health. Third, James Campbell Quick thanks the University of Texas at Arlington for the Faculty Development Leave (2000–2001) which was instrumental in the early stages of his executive health research. The authors would like to thank a number of family, friends, and colleagues who have helped in a wide variety of ways as this work has developed: David J. Gavin, Sheri Schember Quick, Joel Quintans, Ruth Quillian-Wolever, Elena Radeva, David Sampson, Christopher Shook, Kevin Waters, MD. We would like to especially thank Sheila Puffer and her editorial team, especially Bob Ford and Jack Veiga, at the *Academy of Management Executive* for their active support in the development of the special issue (May 2000) on executive health. The opinions expressed are those of the authors and do not necessarily reflect the views of the University of Texas or the World Health Organization.

Foreword

In reading *The Financial Times Guide to Executive Health* for the first time, I was struck by the many examples of executives who have suffered extreme stress in their personal or business lives that potentially had severe consequences for themselves and their com-panies. In most cases they coped successfully without negative implications. However, in some instances the executives suffered serious health and performance problems, and in the most extreme cases, such as those of J. Clifford Baxter (p. 50) and Admiral Jeremy Michael Boorda (p.156), they committed suicide.

By the very nature of their responsibilities, executives are particularly vulnerable to the ravages of stress. The higher up the structural pyramid they reside in an organization, the greater their responsibility and accountability. At the top of the pyramid, the chief executive officer is ultimately responsible for the performance of the business. It is here that the "buck stops," and it is here that it is the loneliest. The CEO makes the tough decisions that affect the lives and well being of his employees – to hire or not hire, to promote or not promote, to fire or not fire. In today's world, "right sizing," often resulting in significant layoffs, is common-place, with potentially devastating results on those affected. Indeed, the job of the CEO, and that of others in the executive suite, is an awesome responsibility.

I became the CEO of a company in distress in 1986. In the ensuing three years, I engineered two layoffs involving hundreds of people. I also dismissed some of my closest friends and colleagues knowing that they would have a difficult time finding other employment. In the most tragic incident, our human resources officer responsible for executing the layoffs died of a stroke, which I believe was at least partially induced by stress. In the process of trying to save the company, I experienced many of the symptoms of severe stress discussed in this book, including sleep-less nights, isolation, loneliness, despair, and hopelessness. Through this experience, I learned that mental and physical fitness is the key to survival. Fortunately, my life was reasonably well balanced between work,

family, and other interest, and I was able to draw upon a reservoir of physical conditioning from a lifetime of swimming and running. In crisis, my wife was my most trusted confidant and advisor; and, even during the worst of times, I maintained a regular regime of running, which helped keep my stress level within tolerable limits.

I congratulate the *Financial Times* and the authors for providing this outstanding guide for business leaders, aspiring executives, and managers who want to learn about the survival skills of the fittest. It would have been particularly useful to me as I faced the challenges in my business.

This book is about winning, not just in business, but also in life. As the authors so ably point out, there are four dimensions to fitness and health that assure winning the game of survival. These four dimensions and the many skills they embody are so clearly discussed that the reader grasps well the importance of mind, body, spirit, and character.

What some business leaders fail to recognize are the pitfalls of blind ambition that lead to neglect of family, health, and the other dimensions of a healthy life. High goals, hard work, and unbridled ambition are exalted attributes in the world of business. However even the healthiest executives can confront circumstances and events which are both daunting and stressful.

The Financial Times Guide to Executive Health is a valuable guide to those who want to win, achieve, and succeed in their chosen fields of business without losing their families or their health. We can all learn from the rich case examples of business leaders who come alive through the pages in this book, from the Morgans to the Rockefellers, from Bill Gates to Kathryn Graham.

Using the concepts presented by the authors will help your performance at work, while enhancing your heath. This executive health "Bible" should be on every executive and aspiring executive's bookshelf, and in his traveling briefcase.

> **Joseph M. "Jody" Grant**
> **Dallas, Texas**
> **August 2002**

Foreword

I hesitate to write this foreword in case anyone should think I put myself forward as a model of physical and psychological wellbeing.

A small photograph to accompany this article would quickly clear up any misunderstandings on that front!

I am writing this sitting on a plane at 3 a.m. and it's my tenth flight in nine days, providing as good an example as any as to why this book is needed. On reading *The FT Guide to Executive Health*, it immediately struck me as an original, practical and, best of all, useful contribution to management. It contains the sort of knowledge and advice which, years later, you realize should have been offered to you at Business School – but wasn't.

I can think of several course modules I would happily have traded for one like this.

As in all fields of endeavour – sport, art, scholarship – being the best in the world is a lot more physically and mentally demanding than being the best in, for example, a small town. The sort of intense physical and mental preparation we see in top sportsmen might seem inappropriate to a business manager, but I believe it's as important. I find it helpful that a basic premise of the book is to accept the pressures of modern business, instead of railing against them, it helps the reader to do something about it.

The authors bring together apparently disparate facets of management life, physical health, relationships, leadership style, and integrity, creating a powerful connection between them, with a strong message for us all.

As you might imagine, the book has given me a fresh determination to improve. Please don't judge the book on my efforts!

Terry Leahy
20 May, 2002

Part I

Your greatest asset: managing health for success

1

Competition, conflict, and executive health

Yes, often the days were full of "stress and strain," he said in old age, "full of care, full of anxiety, it is true, and yet full of happiness that words cannot express: happiness because we were accomplishing from the earliest of our business experience, we were triumphing over the difficulties; we were being strengthened and prepared to meet the larger responsibilities."

John D. Rockefeller Sr
Founder of Standard Oil
A reflection on building the business in the late 1880s

Health is a state of complete physical, mental and social well-being, and not merely the absence of disease or infirmity.

The World Health Organization, Constitution, 1948

John D. Rockefeller Sr's obsession with work and worry while building his business led to stress, strain, and very serious health problems by the time he was fifty years old. Had Mr Rockefeller not made a number of life changes to enhance his health, he may well not have lived into his late 90s. The struggle he faced in balancing his ambitious striving with care of his health remains an ageless challenge for executives. However, there are at least three reasons why executive and managerial health has become an especially important leading-edge issue today. First, the terrain of the new competitive landscape has increased the performance pressures and job insecurities to which executives and managers are subject. Second, executives and managers play key roles in the creation of economic benefits and wealth, not only for themselves and their families, but also for a wide range of beneficiaries throughout an entire society. Third, there are a variety of economic and organizational risks and costs associated with executive and managerial disability and death, for which not only executives, managers, and their families, but also a wider range of constituencies, pay a price.

Globalization, complexity, and change

Executives in a vice-grip

The health of executives around the world is at risk as a result of two opposing forces placing them in a vice-grip. These opposing forces are competitive pressure and job insecurity. There is a significant increase in competitive pressures to which organizations and executives are subject coupled with greater unpredictability of these pressures. That is, given the emergence of the new economy and the continuing shifts in the old economy, economic and competitive pressures can be very hard for business managers and executives to forecast and predict. While these competitive pressures are escalating and shifting, there is an accompanying increase in the job insecurity experienced by many managers and executives.

Overlaid on these two opposing forces that have managers and executives in a vice-grip is an accelerating rate of complexity and change in business. The new economy best reflects the increasing complexity of business environments, with the boom of the dot com companies during 1999 and the dramatic decline of many of these same companies during 2000. This decline in the technology sector of the financial markets was an important contributing force for the slumping broader markets during the year, introducing an unwelcome volatility to both individual and corporate financial stability. Advances in technology have also been instrumental in the increased complexity of business. No longer does an automotive mechanic fit the grease-covered stereotype of a generation ago. Rather, that automotive mechanic may well be a master's-educated software expert who can read automotive diagnostic equipment to pinpoint engine problems in the same way a cardiologist reads an echo-cardiogram to check an executive's heart.

> If the high-tech sector in the global macroeconomic village is driving the increasing complexity of business, it is also driving the rate of change in business.

If the high-tech sector in the global macroeconomic village is driving the increasing complexity of business, it is also driving the rate of change in business. This accelerating rate of change is reflected in technological advances, especially in communication and information technology, which can lead to rather dramatic market-share shifts for major companies over relatively short periods of time. For example, Microsoft's competitors at various times had majority shares of the browser market only to see 20 to 30 percent shifts in market share over one-to-two-year periods wipe out their positions. The changes in the old economy sectors of business may not be quite as rapid and dramatic, yet they also are occurring.

John Chain, Commander in Chief of the Strategic Air Command in the late 1980s, suggested at the time that one would have to reach back to the time of Martin Luther to find an era in human history as fertile with the potential for significant change. The end of the Cold War and the fall of the Iron Curtain laid the groundwork for this period of significant change and also opened wide the gates for a second great period of globalization. The first great period of globalization preceded World War I and saw waves of Europeans, especially eastern Europeans, flood into the eastern United States. These men and women took up jobs in the steel and related industries, helping to fuel America's economic rise to become what is now the center of a global macroeconomic village.

Margaret Thatcher and globalization

The current period of globalization has created a major restructuring of the competitive landscape for a wide range of industries, and this restructuring is ongoing. Margaret Thatcher was a symbolic and substantive driving force for this period of globalization. As the British politician who captured the leadership of the Conservative Party in 1975 from Winston Churchill's protégés, Thatcher made two speeches filled with militant hostility to the Communist Party in 1976. This won her the name "Iron Lady" from the Russians and established her global identity. She went on to become Prime Minister in 1979, led the British in the Falkland War in 1983, and transformed the British economy into a much more competitive economic system. While symbolic of this era of globalization and rapid expansion of free enterprise, a number of Thatcher's policies and their effects carried social costs. For example, the divorce rate in the United Kingdom during the pre-Thatcher years was the lowest in the European Union (EU) while in the post-Thatcher years the divorce rate in the UK rose to the highest in the EU. Thatcher was a driving force for the privatization of many British industries during the 1980s, a process that helped usher in a markedly more competitive industrial landscape in the United Kingdom.

As markets are opening up all around the world, it is increasingly difficult for a manager, executive, or organization to identify a safe harbor protected from the ongoing sea changes that buffet most industries and economic sectors. Increased globalization has been accompanied by a corresponding increase in global interdependency, carrying with it both an upside and a downside. For example, advances in the high-tech sectors helped fuel job creation in Europe during the late 1990s. However, when the restructuring and downturn came in 2000, the interdependencies across economies put many people out of work. While the US economy accounted for about 35 percent of world economic activity after World War II, its global role moved back toward its historical place of about 16 percent as the European and Japanese economies were rebuilt. However, by 2000, US gross domestic product accounted for almost 30 percent of world output, up from 26 percent in 1992. Further, US companies make almost 50 percent of all world corporate profits, which is a 33 percent increase in a decade. Globalization in the 1990s has also made US companies much more dependent on overseas revenues.

Competition and conflict

Globalization and the opening of markets spawned by the end of the Cold War set the stage for head-to-head competition in core industries among the economies of Japan, Europe, and America. The increase in competition has led to a different kind of warfare, waged not by national military forces but by multinational corporations. While the health risks associated with military warfare are rather well understood, both in terms of the physical risks of loss of life or limb and the psychological risks of combat stress and battle fatigue, the health risks associated with corporate warfare are less well understood. Where corporate warfare degenerates into workplace violence, physical threats, and executive kidnappings, it more closely parallels the landscape of military warfare operations. Both military warfare and corporate warfare are based on a limited-resource world view, in which there is competition for scarce resources, whether land and raw materials or populations and economic markets.

Two health-related effects

Competition and conflict have two health-related effects on managers and executives. The first effect is the fight-or-flight response, especially pronounced in males, which is the physiological arousal associated with competition and pressure. Competition has a natural tendency to elicit the experience of threat and potential loss, both of which are highly stressful. Sustained, prolonged competition and pressure may lead to chronic fight reactions in managers and executives, which include elevated heart rates, muscle tension, depressed immune system activity, and elevated blood pressures. While the short-term effects of these physical changes are highly adaptive in dealing with legitimate emergencies and in achieving peak performances, they have debilitating long-term effects and expose managers and executives to a wide range of medical and psychological health risks, such as cardiovascular disease, depression, and anxiety. Some of these health risks are highly lethal, as Jerry Junkins unfortunately found in the midst of a major corporate downsizing of Texas Instruments (TI) in 1996. As chairman, CEO, and president of TI, Mr Junkins was leading the corporate downsizing and restructuring when he prematurely and unexpectedly suffered a fatal heart attack in Stuttgart, Germany. The fight-or-flight response, therefore, may have acute effects on managers and executives who are in the midst of intense competitive and/or conflicted work environments.

The second effect of competition and conflict is subtler and less pronounced, yet has just as adverse long-term health consequences. This is the experience of social isolation and the loneliness of command. Managers and executives are structurally in positions of command and responsibility in organizational life, which implies exclusion from membership in the rank and file. The physical effects of social isolation and loneliness tend to be chronic and progressive rather than acute. The loss of social integration and psychological intimacy may overwhelm the manager or executive who is not able to overcome the communication barriers that can result. Such isolation can lead to the experience of desperation that may precipitate suicide, as was the case for John Curtis Jr in 1997, only months after he had taken the helm of Luby's as a new CEO (see Chapter 3).

> The loss of social integration and psychological intimacy may overwhelm the manager or executive who is not able to overcome the communication barriers that can result.

People, profits, and employment downsizing: the paradox

One might argue that these are isolated cases of individual executives who cannot cope with the pressures of competition. This view fails to recognize our collective humanity, and it fails also to recognize the coming shortfall of executives and managers forecast by the American Management Association. Our future rests on our ability to be productive while at the same time caring for people. When the collision of people and profits strikes the executive boardroom, it strikes at the heart of the free enterprise system. While some would argue that people and profits do collide, we call that perspective into question.

One of the most common organizational strategies used by executives during the 1990s for coping with competitive pressure was employment downsizing aimed at enhancing financial performance and organizational efficiency. Employment downsizing (that is, reducing employment by 5 percent or more) is not the route to financial success. In other words, cutting people does not help profits. Alternatively, Cascio and his colleagues (1997) did find evidence that asset restructuring can lead to enhanced financial performance. Rather than leading to an organization that is lean and mean, employment downsizing more often leads to an organization that is lean and weak. The extreme of this case was Union Carbide's operations in Bhopal, India, which were so weakened that when the 1985 crisis hit, it overwhelmed the capacity of local management to address the problem. In terms of death rate, Bhopal became the worst industrial accident in history despite the best intentions and efforts, after the fact, of Union Carbide CEO Warren Anderson and other corporate executives and managers to rescue the situation. (For more on Bhopal, see Chapter 5.)

While managers and executives are facing an era of enhanced competition with its associated pressures and job insecurity, business activities have always been competitive. John D. Rockefeller Sr experienced the inevitable stress, competition, and challenge of becoming a business success that every generation of business men and women have faced. Rockefeller's description of the stress and strain of his early business years, as set out in the opening lines of this chapter, captures well the businessperson's angst. In his particular case, he became a stunning business success who, by the age of 33, became the first millionaire in the world and who, by the age of 43, owned the largest monopoly in the world, the Standard Oil Company. However, the same extraordinary imbalance that led to his financial success placed his health at risk, and by the age of 53 John D. Rockefeller Sr was nearly bankrupt in his health accounts. He was fortunate not to have died prematurely at that age and, in fact, engaged in a series of life-balancing activities that enhanced his health and extended his life for an additional 45 years. John D. Rockefeller Sr lived to the age of 98.

An epidemic? the stress test

Rockefeller clearly passed the stress test in his life, if that test measures longevity. He lived well past his life expectancy at birth, which would have been approximately 45 years. Could Rockefeller pass the stress test today? The American Institute of Stress calls job stress a health epidemic, based on a set of indicators, including self-report surveys, unscheduled absence data, violent incidents at work, and job loss numbers. The 2001 Labor Day survey by the Marlin Company in collaboration with the American Institute of Stress found 35 percent responding that their jobs are harming their physical and emotional health; 50 percent of employees reporting a more demanding workload than a year earlier; and 42 percent indicating that job pressures are interfering with their personal relationships. As early as 1980, the National Institute for Occupational Safety and Health (NIOSH) identified stress and psychological disorders in the workplace as one of the top ten occupational health hazards in America. Layoffs and downsizing continued through the 1990s. Restructuring even led to "management massacres" in the 1980s, (Sanderschein, Schein, 1986). Are executives in the midst of an epidemic?

Translated literally from the Greek, epidemic means "upon the people." Epidemiology is the basic science and most fundamental practice of public health and preventive medicine. Epidemics of infection are often assessed on the basis of three indicators:

1. the percent of the population affected by the disease

2. the rate of spread of the disease

3. the intensity of the adverse impact of the disease.

While the ancients often lacked adequate knowledge to do more than observe victims and record mortality, the evolution of preventive medicine from the mid-1800s affords greater power to stop epidemics. Whereas treatment alone is rarely effective in the management of epidemics, prevention is essential in the war on any epidemic. By some accounts, the war is being won if we use the broader American social demographic data as an indicator.

Contrary to the *Business Week* headline "Stress: The Test Americans Are Failing," Americans are passing the stress test when life expectancy is the operational measure. American men and women extended their average life expectancy at birth by over 50 percent in less than a century, from less than 50 years in 1900 to over 75 years by the mid-1980s (*Vital Statistics of the United States*, 1988). Certainly some stress is good; not all stress is bad. The stress response is a normal psychophysiological response to stressful or traumatic events, environmental demands, and interpersonal conflicts. In spite of this normalcy of the stress response, stress poses a risk to health when it is experienced too frequently, too intensely, or for too prolonged a period of time, or when the stress-induced energy is mismanaged. Unfortunately, stress is still a contributing cause, directly or indirectly implicated in over 50 percent of all human morbidity and mortality (Cooper, Quick, 1999). In the United States and all developed countries, the ten leading causes of death account for about 80 percent of all deaths. Stress is directly implicated in four of the top ten causes (heart disease, strokes, injuries, and suicide and homicide) and indirectly implicated in a further three (cancer, chronic liver disease, and emphysema and chronic bronchitis). This is the broader social-demographic context in which executive health must be considered, but life and death are not the only important issues.

Executives and economic activity

> Not only do lower socioeconomic and occupational statuses have higher mortality rates; they also have higher incidences of high blood pressure, smoking and other health risks.

Executives play a central role in the creation of economic activity and wealth within a society. Their comparatively lower mortality and morbidity rates have been documented for centuries, a fact that benefits many within society. Higher mortality rates for lower socioeconomic levels have been found for both individuals and national populations alike. Not only do lower socioeconomic and occupational statuses have higher mortality rates; they also have higher incidences of high blood pressure, smoking and other health risks. These data are used by some to argue that our primary collective concern should be with the well-being of the poor, the disenfranchised, and the unemployed. While we recognize that the mark of a great society may be how well it treats the least of its members, we also recognize the central and critical role executives play in creating, enhancing, advancing, and maintaining the economic wealth of a nation.

In his inquiry into the wealth of nations, Adam Smith was concerned with the productive use of labor and with the leveraging effects of technology, as well as other topics and issues. We concur and in addition suggest that executive health is a contemporary factor that contributes to the wealth of a nation. Research on upper echelons and top management teams shows their positive effects on the success of the firm, and by extension the creation of wealth. For example, Jack Welch created an additional $52 billion of market value during his tenure as CEO of General Electric (GE), and Roberto Goizueta created $59 billion during his tenure as CEO of Coca-Cola (Morris, 2001).

Balancing love and work

A central theme in our research and writing is balance. We are referring to balance along a number of dimensions of living to enhance health. These include balance in work and non-work activities, in effortful and effortless activities, in tension and in relaxation, in the muscle tension of the flexor and the extensor muscle groups, and in giving and receiving in relationships with other people. Hippocrates is the Greek physician credited with being the father of medicine, and among his early formulations was the importance of balance in the body as a way to avoid illness and to enhance health.

Freud captured the notion of balance in his response to the question of what constitutes a happy, healthy life. His response was love and work. There is a need for mastery and for productive activity, which are good for people, just as there is a need for nurturance and for loving relationships with other people. Balancing the head and the heart does not mean necessarily a 50–50 arrangement, or a 60–40 arrangement. Balance does mean that the executive's need to achieve must be gratified, and the executive's need to be cared for and nurtured must also be gratified. Dr Smiley Blanton addressed the importance of this central life issue in his book *Love or Perish*. His thesis was that it is imperative for individuals in their mature adulthoods to love other people, invest their time and energy in others, and care for others, lest they risk suffering the serious health consequences, including premature death, of not doing so.

Executive health: security through strength

On turning 50 recently, an information technology executive told us he was reminded of the old quip: "If I had known I was going to live this long, I would have taken better care of myself." Fortunately in his case, he is quite healthy, happy, and productive, having now outlived his father by 14 years. There are real advantages for those managers and executives who safeguard their health for the long run. Once John D. Rockefeller Sr began doing so, he nearly doubled his life span and neared the century mark in an era when that was quite unusual.

In facing the Soviet threat in the 1980s, US President Ronald Reagan and UK Prime Minister Margaret Thatcher pursued the same strategy, which was security through strength. We believe the same message applies to individual managers, executives, and their organizations with regard to executive health. Managers and executives also achieve security through strength.

We use a preventive medicine paradigm for our executive health model (see Figure 1.1). This paradigm involves enhancing strength factors while eliminating, reducing, and/or managing health risk factors. We understand these two sets of factors as the key determinants of executive health. The model also includes the key personal and organizational outcomes of executive health. In addition, we aim to contribute to an emerging focus on positive health, which goes beyond simple disease prevention or the absence of illness.

Executive health incorporates physical, psychological, spiritual, and ethical well-being. Each of these four health dimensions contributes to an executive's strength and security. When each health dimension is strong, executives can be most effective as individuals, as managers, as peers and colleagues, and as leaders within their organizations.

Personal and organizational outcomes

Executive health has consequences, which manifest both personal and organizational outcomes. First is individual vitality, which is the power to live with mental and physical vigor. Second is low morbidity and mortality, which are low levels of disease and death. Third is organizational health, defined as high performance, adaptability, and flexibility throughout the firm. High levels of executive health along all four dimensions contribute to individual vitality, low morbidity, and low mortality rates at the individual level. In addition, high levels of executive health within an

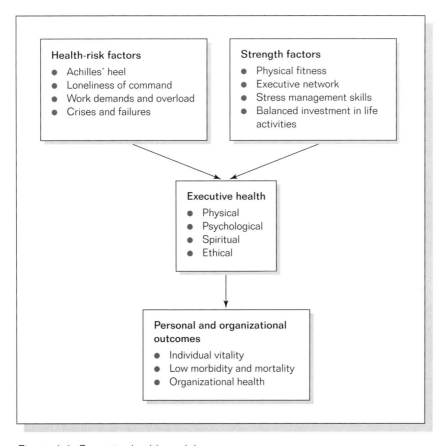

Figure 1.1 Executive health model

Source: J. C. Quick, J. H. Gavin, C. L. Cooper & J. D. Quick. "Executive health: building strength and managing risks", *Academy of Management Executive*, 14, Figure 1. ©2000 Reproduced with permission of *The Academy of Management*

organization contribute to organizational health. Our primary focus is to chart a course toward the achievement of excellent executive health through building strength while managing risks, thus ensuring success in these personal and organizational outcomes.

Four dimensions of executive health

Physical well-being, the first dimension of executive health, is influenced by biological inheritance and physical fitness. While an executive's biological inheritance cannot be altered, it can be managed by knowing the endowments and vulnerabilities that lie within it. Complete physical fitness includes cardiovascular fitness, musculoskeletal strength, and muscular flexibility. These complementary aspects of physical well-being collectively serve as the foundation from which psychological, spiritual, and ethical well-being can grow.

Among the greatest risks for executives is cardiovascular disease; heart attacks have killed suddenly several leading American, Japanese, and other nations' executives over the years. Heart disease is the leading cause of death in the United States and all developed countries. Among the risk factors for coronary heart disease are hypertension, smoking, diet, diabetes, physical inactivity, and a family history of heart disease. Physical well-being reduces the exposure to heart attacks and other fatal as well as nonfatal medical conditions that place an executive's health at risk.

Psychological well-being, the second dimension of executive health, is the ability to deal constructively with reality, the capacity to adapt to change, the capacity to love, and the ability to direct one's emotional energy toward creative and constructive outlets. Executives' psychological well-being affects their decision-making ability. To make a good decision requires the ability to evaluate the situation, to consider everyone's needs and interests with a clear vision of reality, and to act decisively. Executives' ability to cognitively process information and to provide clear and accurate interpretations for decision-making is critical. Thus a high level of psychological well-being among an organization's executives enhances their ability to make good decisions, which in turn increases the health of the organization. Diminished psychological health among executives may weaken, if not destroy, an organization.

Psychological well-being also influences an executive's ability to develop interpersonal support, an essential aspect of well-being. A strong network of social support enhances positive health and decreases levels of illness and death. For optimal emotional health, executives need support among those peers with whom they are able to feel comfortable and at ease in open and honest communication. Opportunities to share fears, thoughts, and concerns can be instrumental to psychological health in difficult times.

Spiritual vitality is a more elusive dimension of executive health, and its effects are often overlooked. Difficult times often remind executives who are spiritually alive that there is more to life than the current challenge. They are aware of a greater purpose in life. In addition to a more global view to their personal lives, spiritually whole executives move beyond themselves to embrace the needs and desires of others. They recognize their ability to go beyond the basic functions of the organization, using their positions and power to enhance the lives of the organization's members and the community as a whole. Some executives have attained a level of spiritual vitality that has allowed them, personally and through their organizations, to effect change for everyone. US President Bush has made serious efforts to recognize and integrate into the larger culture faith-based efforts for care giving. Accommodating religion and spirituality in the workplace is a very contemporary concern for many.

Andrew Carnegie is one great example of a spiritually vital executive. In June of 1889, the *North American Review* published his article entitled "Wealth." An editorial response to his article in December of the same year coined the term "The Gospel of Wealth." Carnegie defended great wealth as an inevitable outcome of the capitalist system, and he claimed that wealth could be beneficial, provided the amasser of the wealth regarded himself as but a steward responsible for returning that fortune to the society out of which it came. Through his many philanthropic endeavors, Carnegie gave away over $350 million during his lifetime. Bill Gates and Ted Turner are contemporary businessmen whose philanthropy may rival the standard set by Carnegie.

Ethical character completes the foundation from which the healthy executive can function. Character is who you are when no one is watching (Murray, 1998). Character is the personal code that provides the strength and insight to make ethically sound decisions, especially in difficult situations. Like psychological well-being, character is essential to effective

> Ethical character allows executives to make difficult decisions in the short run in order to ensure the best outcomes for all in the long run.

executive decision-making. Executives' commitment to the ethical actions of the organization, especially in the face of difficult choices, is of critical importance to the continued success of the organization and all of its stakeholders. Ethical character allows executives to make difficult decisions in the short run in order to ensure the best outcomes for all in the long run. Executives' character gives them the strength to make right decisions even when faced with the likelihood of immediate negative feedback.

In addition to Andrew Carnegie, another example of a man of strong ethical character is Milton Hershey. At the turn of the century, he built a company, as well as a community around that company, so all could share in his dream and success. In addition to the business complex, Hershey built a town with all of the accoutrements of a large city. The town of

Hershey, Pennsylvania was complete with the Hershey hospital, theater, park, college, and orphanage. But what really makes the story of Milton Hershey important is his strength of character in the face of the Great Depression. Although the revenue of the company plummeted to a low of $21 million in 1933, half of its 1929 peak, Hershey made sure that his townspeople didn't suffer. He maintained the rigid production schedule, cutting no wages and discharging no employees. Instead, in the face of these difficult times, he fought the depression with his own building campaign, spending more than $10 million on improving the city, adding attractions to the town to draw tourists, and expanding the factory to add more jobs. Milton Hershey placed the future of the people and the town above his own financial security.

Building strength and managing health risks

The core of our thinking about executive health rests on the basic assumption that executive health is a dynamic or idealized goal which is sought, rather than an end state at which one arrives. That is, healthy executives always seek to improve their health and well-being. As we have observed, the executive health model in Figure 1.1 suggests an executive's state of physical, psychological, spiritual, and ethical health is optimized through an ongoing process of managing risks and building strength. Executives can build strength through a process of identifying inheritance endowments, complemented with acquiring skills and activities aimed at building on one's strengths.

Executives can also manage health risks through a process of identifying threats to their health and then taking appropriate steps to guard against the threat or risk having an adverse impact. For example, one survey of executives found that alcohol consumption and travel headed the list of factors contributing to executive health problems (Veiga, 2000). An essential element of preventive medicine is the early identification of such health risk factors before they unfold into asymptomatic physical or psychological disorders (e.g., blocked arteries without chest pains or shortness of breath on exertion) or, worse yet, into symptomatic diseases, disorders, or behavioral problems (e.g., a heart attack). Adapting this preventive medicine approach to our model of executive health suggests that executives' first step is to develop a good knowledge of the genetic, inherited, acquired, and environmental factors that may threaten their health and well-being.

While important health-risk factors may be genetic or inherited, another set of health-risk factors is environmental in nature. Some organizations and work environments either tolerate and/or encourage dysfunctional behavior, defined as motivated behavior by an employee that has negative consequences for individuals, groups, and/or the organization itself (Griffin *et al.*, 1998). Other organizations are toxic in ways that cause people emotional pain and suffering. Management professor Peter Frost suggests that those executives and managers who shoulder the sadness and the anger endemic to many organizations, helping to metabolize their emotional pain and suffering, are organizational heroes who place themselves at risk in terms of their own health and well-being (Frost, Robinson, 1999).

Outline of the book

This book has four parts and ten chapters aimed at helping executives and managers better understand their vulnerabilities and the threats to their health as well as their strength and power. Part I is composed of this first chapter, which sets out a framework for understanding executive and managerial health and why it is especially important in these challenging times. An executive's health is his or her greatest personal asset, for without it all else may be lost.

Part II of the book focuses on the threats to health that managers and executives face. One key to healthy living is risk management. Work life is inevitably risky, offering both great benefits as well as dangers and threats to one's health. Risk identification is the first step to risk management. This part of the book is composed of four chapters. Chapter 2 discusses the executive's Achilles' heel, which is an executive's inherited or acquired vulnerability, and the five major health risks which executives face in today's world. Chapter 3 examines the loneliness of command, which inevitably accompanies life at the top of one's organization and/or profession. Chapter 4 reviews the work demands and travel stress executives face. Chapter 5 concludes this part of the book and examines coping with crises and failures. Identifying the early warning signs of problems or dangers is among the best preventive action that an executive can take in protecting health, ensuring balanced, long-term achievement and success, and preventing serious health problems and disabilities.

Part III is the second major part of the book and emphasizes the proactive steps that executives and managers can take to strengthen and balance each of the four dimensions of executive health. Chapter 6 examines physical health as the cornerstone for executive strength and performance. Chapter 7 addresses psychological well-being, with consideration given to both cognitive thinking and emotional feeling. Chapter 8 raises the issue of spiritual vitality in a broader context than a religious or denominational framework. Chapter 9 discusses ethics in the workplace and the centrality of good character to healthy living.

Part IV concludes the book with an emphasis on the self-reliant executive who is interdependent in personal relationships and professional collaborations. The self-reliant executive balances attention to the dual needs to achieve and to succeed on the one hand while maintaining his or her health and well-being on the other hand.

Chapter 1 in a nutshell

1. Executives and managers are in the midst of a major period of globalization that is placing them in the vice-grip of competitive pressures and job insecurity.

2. This period in business is characterized by a constant rate of change and conflict.

3. The vice-grip and constant change are placing managers and executives at risk, yet it is debatable whether they are caught in the midst of a job stress epidemic.

4. Managers and executives play a central role in economic activity and the creation of wealth and economic benefits for many.

5. Managers and executives can find security through strength by developing all dimensions of their health: physical, psychological, spiritual, and ethical.

Part II

Risky business: threats to executive health

2

The Achilles' heel:
risk and vulnerability

My only job in life is to stay healthy.

Jack Welch, CEO of GE, March 30, 2001
in anticipation of retirement

It's true hard work never killed anybody, but I figure, why take the chance?

Ronald Reagan, US President, April 22, 1987
to the annual Gridiron Dinner

Globalization and competition have increased the pressure and stress on executives, managers, and employees at work. Pressure and stress, however, are not necessarily bad nor unhealthy. Stress can be the spice of life as well as the kiss of death. Stress can challenge a person or an organization to high achievement and peak performance, as in the case of the Harley Davidson self-revitalization at the end of the 1980s, when the organization was struggling for its survival. Thus, stress may enhance performance and, in appropriate doses, stress may also enhance health.

There is another side to pressure and stress, because it can enhance health risks and vulnerability, leading to a variety of health problems, including medical, behavioral, and psychological. While Jack Welch seemed to be in robust health and fitness as he approached retirement in 2001, he had also undergone an angioplasty procedure in 1995 to open his arteries and preclude further cardiovascular problems, such as a heart attack.

Texas Instruments chairman and CEO Jerry R. Junkins was not so fortunate as Mr Welch. TI was a booming organization in the early 1990s, with its stock price increasing 500 percent over a five-year period from 1990 through September 1995, ending at over $10 a share from a beginning price of about $2 per share. Then TI hit a very difficult business stretch, and Mr Junkins had to engage in a difficult and draining restructuring of the company. A fitness buff and very likable person, Mr Junkins became drained by the restructuring and downsizing, as well as by a slide in the stock price, in which TI lost over 40 percent of its value in just over six months. It was at the end of this major downsizing that Mr Junkins had a heart attack on Wednesday, May 29, 1996, while riding in a car in Stuttgart, Germany. He died prematurely at the age of 58, with no known personal or family risk factors for heart disease.

One might say that Mr Junkins did not die in vain, though that is small comfort for close colleagues, loved ones and family. From a business low at the time of his death, TI enjoyed a four-year resurgence as reflected in an eight-fold increase in the stock price from $6 to $48 per share. Let us suggest, however, that Mr Junkins need not have died. The key focus of this chapter is to explore an executive's Achilles' heel, with the risk and vulnerability that it creates. When stress is brought to bear upon the weak link in an executive's armor, there is the risk that the blow will be telling, if not fatal as in Mr Junkins's case. However, we begin first with a brief discussion of stress, performance, and achievement.

Stress, performance, and achievement

Many people, especially executives, regard stress as a bad word, and they prefer to use a word such as "challenge" for positive stress. Hans Selye, the physician who popularized the stress concept, chose the word *eustress*, which may be defined as the healthy, positive, constructive outcome of stressful events and the stress response. The relationship between stress and performance has been known since 1908, when Robert Yerkes and James Dodson demonstrated increased performance under conditions of arousal up to an optimal point, as shown in Figure 2.1.

As the figure shows, performance increases with increasing stress loads up to an optimum point, and then the stress load becomes too

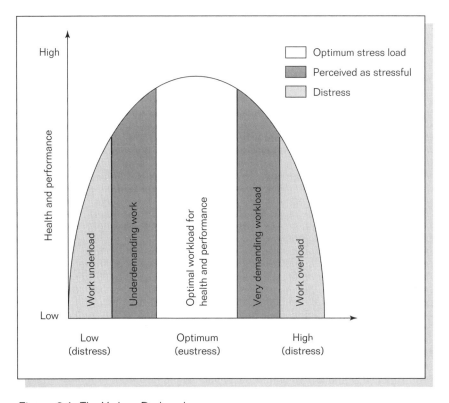

Figure 2.1 The Yerkes–Dodson law

great, resulting in depressed performance. The optimum stress load that maximizes performance varies by individual and by task, based on several considerations. Individual considerations include susceptibility to stress, fatigue, psychological and cognitive skills, and physical capacity. Task considerations include the complexity, difficulty, duration, and intensity of the work. The interaction, as reflected in the person's familiarity with the task, also affects the shape and size of the particular Yerkes–Dodson curve. Too little stress and arousal often fail to stimulate performance, just as too much stress and arousal can interfere with performance, especially on complex tasks.

A key focus of our approach to executive well-being is on strategies for enhancing healthy stress and discovering ways to seek out that optimum point of peak performance between underachieving and overstressing along the curve. Excellent health and well-being can be maintained along with high levels of achievement. This is the aim of executive health programs, such as the Duke Executive Health Program in their Center for

Living. The first part of the Duke Executive Health Program is a personalized assessment tailored to the executive's life and work styles. Health planning and strategies are then designed to manage against the health risks and vulnerabilities identified in the personalized assessment.

Risk and vulnerability

One of the myths of American culture is the John Wayne myth. This myth is not only false; it actually does some injustice to the film legacy of John Wayne. The John Wayne myth says that mature men should be strong, independent, macho, and invulnerable. There are some women who also ascribe to this myth in their effort to be like men. This myth has a tendency to place distance in the relationships between those who embrace it and leads them to deny their own vulnerabilities, weaknesses, and flaws.

> The John Wayne myth says that mature men should be strong, independent, macho, and invulnerable. There are some women who also ascribe to this myth in their effort to be like men.

Only when these vulnerabilities, weaknesses, and flaws are accepted and understood, however, can resources, strategies, tools, and interpersonal relationships be brought to bear to help the executive in need.

This myth also does not do justice to John Wayne and his film legacy. A careful review of John Wayne's western and war movies shows that invariably Wayne is surrounded by a close band of supporters who are fighting for right, justice, and the American way. This is a band of heroic figures who together strengthen each other and overcome challenging odds to win out. This storyline and cast of heroic figures also have applicability in the business world. When the Chrysler Corporation was first struggling for its survival in the early 1980s, the company hired former Ford executive Lee Iacocca. Mr Iacocca did not go into Chrysler as the Lone Ranger (whom, incidentally, John Wayne never portrayed), bent on saving the company single-handedly. That would have been foolhardy and risky. Rather, Mr Iacocca took a chapter from the real John Wayne and handpicked a team of experts, among whom were many former Ford managers and executives whom he could trust, to take over the company. He later described himself as the general in the war to save Chrysler. He did, and made a ton of money for the US Treasury, which had guaranteed the bank loans that also saved the company.

Where should executives or managers first look to identify their personal risk and vulnerability factors? The very first place to look is in family history, preferably going back several generations, to identify the age of death, cause of death, and major health problems that one's biological ancestors have experienced. We have worked with executives and managers who are adopted and cannot therefore trace their biological family history. This is very unfortunate because the absence of information certainly does not free one from the health risks and problems that existed for those ancestors. A family history health assessment goes a long way to help a manager or executive identify his or her personal Achilles' heel.

The Achilles' heel

An Achilles' heel is a person's particular inherited and/or acquired health vulnerability. The concept of the Achilles' heel comes from Greek mythology and has been applied more recently to the organ inferiority hypothesis in medicine.* This hypothesis states that an individual is susceptible or vulnerable to disease at the weakest organ or system in the body, such as, for some, the cardiovascular system. Harold Wolff, a pioneering physician in psychosomatic medicine, was primarily responsible for framing our understanding of the Achilles' heel concept. Subsequent medical and psychological research has born out Wolff's basic hypothesis, and the study of family history is one rich source of data for identifying a genetic or inherited Achilles' heel. In particular, the study of hypertensive and non-hypertensive people has clearly shown the influence that family medical history may have on health and well-being.

While the Achilles' heel concept can help executives identify health risk and vulnerability factors, it is critical to understand that these are predisposing factors in identifying health risks, not predetermining factors. Thus, just because your father and grandfather both died before the age of 70 does not mean that you will. This distinction is substantive, important, and essential for anyone using health-risk assessment concepts from preventive medicine. While the term "predetermining" suggests a certain inevitability that a health problem or premature death will

---

* The term "Achilles' heel" has become proverbial for referring to a potential weakness. It derives its meaning from Achilles, the most valiant Greek warrior of the Trojan War. The Fates prophesised that Achilles would die in the Trojan War. In fear of this prediction, Thetis bathed her infant in the river Styx to make him immortal. Only the heel by which she held him remained vulnerable to a fatal wound.

result from a health-risk factor, "predisposing" suggests a vulnerability that, if managed and guarded against properly, may never cause a health problem nor premature death.

Family history

For example, the early deaths of his father, a steel industry executive, at age 54, and his grandfather, a trucking industry entrepreneur, at 48, led sales executive James F. Quick Jr to anticipate a life expectancy not to exceed 60. Our dad laid out a life plan that would secure the education of his sons and the financial security of his wife in her later years. These plans were not made with the expectation that he would die at 60, but rather they were contingency plans developed on the basis of the best information of the 1930s and 1940s to ensure the future of those for whom he was responsible. As it turned out, our dad did not need his contingency plan. While his paternal family history suggested that he might not live beyond the age of 60, he actively engaged in strategies and healthy habits designed to enhance his health and well-being. These lifestyle management actions and a program of preventive health management led him to exceed his low-side projected life expectancy by 25 years. He lived productively in retirement to the age of 85, at which time he did in fact leave his wife very financially secure and his sons in the midst of productive and rewarding careers.

Charting out one's family history for health-risk factors is not especially complicated, though it can be difficult at times to get the necessary family history information. We strongly encourage executives and managers to seek out this information for their own long-term health planning. Many managers and executives with whom we have worked over the years simply construct a family tree going back several generations. On each branch of the tree they record the name, age of death, cause of death, and major health problems for the given family member. There are often some missing people or bits of information, but this tends not to be highly critical. The core of what is being sought is the big picture. When an executive is able to chart 24 to 36 family members from previous generations, a pattern often emerges that shows either a very long-lived history with few health problems, or one in which a number of people have died of such ailments as heart disease or cancer at relatively early ages.

Executive health risks

What are the major health problems for which executives are at risk? We identify five major health risks that should be of paramount concern to executives, managers, and their organizations. These include both psychological and medical health problems. In addition, there are lesser known health problems and unique vulnerabilities that may emerge from an executive's personalized health-risk assessment. An executive should not discount these lesser-known health problems, because they may be just as devastating and lethal as those that are more common. Therefore, we focus attention first on the major health risks based on epidemiological, medical, and psychological research evidence. Executives and managers should couple this general health-risk information with a much more detailed understanding of their personal history, family history, and particular environmental circumstances.

The five major health risks that we address first are:

● workaholism and burnout

● depression and anxiety

● physical inactivity

● unhealthy dietary habits

● abuse of tobacco, alcohol or drugs.

Each of these health risks has adverse consequences for an executive or manager, his or her family, and ultimately his or her organization. One of the keys to maintaining excellent health and to recovering from a wide variety of health problems is early diagnosis and intervention. One of the complications for executives and managers with emerging health problems is the denial of early warning signs or symptoms. Because they view their own strength in terms of their ability to exercise positive influence in their organizations and industries, executives may overlook the introspection and self-awareness that are absolutely essential to early awareness of potential problems.

Executives may rely on feedback from others as well. For example, the wife of the chief executive of an oil field service organization with whom we worked was an excellent source of feedback to him concerning his early warning sign of being overstressed, which was irritability. While his managers were reluctant to give him that feedback, his wife was quite comfortable and capable of doing that in order to help him with his health maintenance activities.

Workaholism and burnout

Workaholism

In his highly personal account of workaholism, *The Man who Mistook his Job for a Life*, literary agent and highly successful entrepreneur Jonathon Lazear traces his path through his exhilarating, deal-making pinnacle, to the downward spiral of detachment and disillusionment of workaholism, to his "waking up with the house on fire." He describes his path back to a productive, but balanced relationship with work and – more importantly – the path back to well-being through reconnecting with himself, his partner, his children, and his community.

Hard work is considered a modern virtue. In Europe, the influence of French church reformer John Calvin has led to great value being placed on thrift, industriousness, and hard work. In the United States, this spirit is manifested in the Puritan ethic. Commitment, long hours, high performance standards, job involvement, and reliability ("running a tight ship") are all valuable assets in today's competitive world. In reasonable measure and taken in balance, these characteristics are vital to executive success. Taken to the extreme, these behaviors can become overwhelming and destructive.

"Workaholic" has become a popular term applied to anyone who works many hours or who works very intensively. But when the term was coined by W. E. Oates in the 1960s, it was purposely meant to parallel the compulsive behavior of alcoholics (Porter, 1996). Workaholics are not simply people who work hard or work long hours. Like an alcoholic, a workaholic neglects his or her family, personal relationships, and other responsibilities. Workaholics feel uncomfortable away from work. They are troubled by underlying feelings of inadequacy and work even more in an attempt to increase self-esteem. Also like alcoholics, workaholics live in a state of denial, failing to see the impact of their behavior on family and colleagues, and often trying to hide the addictive behavior – for example, sneaking away from the family during vacation to phone in or to handle correspondence. Workaholics have been called the "respectable addicts" (Killinger, 1991). Table 2.1. provides a self-assessment of workaholic attitudes and behaviors.

Table 2.1 How do you know if you are a workaholic?

---

1. Do you get more excited about your work than about family or anything else?
2. Are there times when you can charge through your work and other times when you can't?
3. Do you take work with you to bed? on weekends? on vacation?
4. Is work the activity you like to do best and talk about most?
5. Do you work more than 40 hours a week?
6. Do you turn your hobbies into money-making ventures?
7. Do you take complete responsibility for the outcome of your work efforts?
8. Have your family or friends given up expecting you on time?
9. Do you take on extra work because you are concerned that it won't otherwise get done?
10. Do you underestimate how long a project will take and then rush to complete it?
11. Do you believe that it is okay to work long hours if you love what you are doing?
12. Do you get impatient with people who have other priorities besides work?
13. Are you afraid that if you don't work hard you will lose your job or be a failure?
14. Is the future a constant worry for you even when things are going very well?
15. Do you do everything energetically and competitively, including play?
16. Do you get irritated when people ask you to stop doing your work in order to do something else?
17. Have your long hours hurt your family or other relationships?
18. Do you think about your work while driving, falling asleep or when others are talking?
19. Do you work or read during meals?
20. Do you believe that more money will solve the other problems in your life?

Source: Reprinted with permission from Workaholics Anonymous, World Service Organization (2002).

Characteristic features of a workaholic include obsessive perfectionism, a high need for control, an irrational commitment to excessive work, an excessive desire to please other people and strong tendency to put their own needs first. Workaholics are the classic over-achievers. When workaholics reach their limits, it affects their work, their family, their friends – their entire well-being. Chronic fatigue, obsessive worry, short temper, mood fluctuations, poor communication, suspiciousness bordering on paranoia, and loss of one's sense of humor and ability to play may all occur. Fear of failure may further erode confidence and increase anxiety. Other addictive behavior such as alcohol or drug abuse may appear. Detachment from children and extramarital affairs are common. At the extreme, loss of integrity, ethical lapses, and dishonesty may occur. (Killinger, 1991; Porter, 1996)

Because of their competence, commitment and hard work, the public lives of workaholics may be filled with success. But their private lives are often a disaster. But, as the experience of Purvis J. Thrash Sr and count-less other CEOs and senior managers attest, it is possible to work hard and to success without the obsessive drive of workaholism.

Purvis J. Thrash Sr – CEO with perspective

Purvis J. Thrash Sr, a petroleum engineer by training, rose through the ranks in the oil industry to becoming president and CEO of Otis Engi-neering Corporation, positions he served for over a decade. Otis Engineering specializes in the design and manufacture of oil field equipment and products. In 1988, Otis Engineering had annual rev-enues of $350 million employed about 4,000 people. Thrash managed Otis Engineering through an unprecedented period of intense com-petition in the oil industry and rapid flunctuations in the worldwide demand for oil field equipment and services. His analytical perspec-tive, effective delegation, careful planning, and strong social support system made him highly effective at work. But he kept work in per-spective. Reflecting on his career at Otis, he commented to us (Quick, Nelson, Quick, 1990)

To me, my family, my friends, my church, my personal enjoyment of life are actually more important to me than my job . . . [I] enjoy life outside of my job, which I think is essential to brining a happy well-rounded man to a chair that must make decisions involving human beings . . . Now there have been times in my career or the career of others where that [long hours] was required. But to my way of thinking that should be a temporary situation based on a peculiar set of circumstances at the time. As a rule, I believe that if an executive is regularly working [that] type of hours there is some kind of problem, probably with management style.

Thrash retired in good health, having kept Otis Engineering highly profitable and contibuting to the value of its parent company, Hal-liburton Company. Clearly, Thrash found success in work, but with balance and perspective.

Burnout

Burnout is a particular risk for executives and is the result of energy loss without recovery. Executives are ambitious and talented individuals who often put forth a great deal of energy as they strive hard to achieve goals, objectives, and outstanding levels of success, either those which they have set for themselves, or those which have been set for them by boards of directors, their bosses, or the dictates of their industrial contexts. There is nothing inherently unhealthy in any of this, whether the ambition, striving, or achievement of laudable goals and objectives. The problem of burnout comes when the executive or manager does not allow for sufficient rest and recovery time from effortful striving and/or does not have the network of supportive relationships from which to draw energy.

Burnout is characterized by emotional exhaustion and an attitude of depersonalization. Emotional exhaustion is the most notable character-istic of burnout, and is essentially the experience of "being out of gas." Brief and temporary periods of emotional depletion are not the same as emotional exhaustion and burnout. Emotional depletion is the natural consequence that follows periods of unusually hard work, strenuous exertion mentally or physically, or great achievement. The executive who recognizes this and allows for recovery time can bounce back to full energy pretty quickly. Burnout sets in when the executive keeps pushing through a period of emotional depletion and into a state of emotional exhaustion. The executive who is out of energy for an extended number of days or weeks is probably entering burnout.

While emotional exhaustion is at the center of the experience of burnout, depersonalization is a second, more negative dimension of burnout. Deper-sonalization is a negative and cynical attitude toward others in the work and home environment. While the emotional exhaustion component leads to the propensity for inactivity, passivity, and lack of responsiveness to work and other people, depersonalization is the active and destructive compo-nent in burnout. Depersonalization leads to caustic comments and barbs that damage rather than build relationships.

Burnout is not simply a psychological problem; it also has notable physical and behavioral dimensions as well. The physical symptoms of burnout can include headaches, physical fatigue, insomnia, loss of weight, and shortness of breath. The behavioral symptoms of burnout can include heightened irritability and expressions of anger, diminished frustration tolerance, increased risk-taking, and moodiness. In the later stages of burnout executives and managers may begin to self-medicate with alcohol or tranquilizers, which then spills into substance-abuse problems. In addition, in the later stages of burnout the executive or manager becomes rigid and inflexible.

Depression and anxiety

Depression

Depression is one of the two most common presenting complaints for stress seen by family physicians (Cooper, Quick, 1999) and has been estimated to take a $70 billion toll annually on businesses (Tanouye, 2001). Depression may be accompanied by extreme anxiety, which we discuss next. Depression as a major executive health risk should be distinguished from the major mental health problem of manic-depressive illness, now known as bipolar disorder. The latter is a physiologically based, often inherited medical problem requiring long-term pharmacological and psychotherapeutic treatment. Bipolar disorder is characterized by periods of great energy, elation, and productivity preceded by and followed by periods of great lethargy, and inactivity. There has been a rather high success rate in the treatment of bipolar disorder, which carries with it the risk of suicide. Therefore, if for no other reason, it warrants ongoing medical and psychological treatment.

In contrast to bipolar disorder, unipolar depression is a health risk in which work, the work environment, and an executive's goals and aspirations are implicated. The high expectations and ambition of executive life are positive attributes often leading to great success and achievement, and which also carry the seeds for depression. The failure to achieve one's stated goals, or failure to help the company achieve its stated goals, leads to the experience of depression. Much has been made at times of Winston Churchill's periods of depression, but these reports are somewhat overblown. An example of a work-related emotional blow that can trigger a depression would be, in Winston Churchill's case, the failure of the military action he directed in the Dardanelles. While most depression is accompanied by the inability to lift oneself out of the experience of misery that interferes with normal life functioning, Churchill in fact resigned his position, took the actions he deemed appropriate to the circumstances, and moved forward with his life.

An executive should make a distinction between 'feeling depressed' and experiencing a depression that requires psychological or medical treatment. Feeling depressed as a result of a major loss, either professionally or personally, is a natural and normal consequence of such an emotional experience. All managers and executives can expect to feel depressed for brief periods of time following such emotional experiences. Depression becomes a health problem when the feelings of depression persist for an extended period of time, when they deepen, and when they interfere with the performance of normal work and personal life activities.

While some depressions appear to have no apparent cause, many depressions are triggered by an emotional blow or dramatic loss to which the executive or manager has an extreme reaction. The triggering event is often, as in Churchill's case, a painful loss. The loss may be in a relationship, such as a close business or professional associate, or a business setback accompanied by material or financial losses. For example, the dramatic failures in many of the technological stocks and businesses in 2000 and 2001, with the accompanying loss of fortunes and accumulation of debts, were fertile ground as triggers for depression in the executives and managers who experienced huge losses. Counterintuitively, depression may also follow great success, with its accompanying elimination of a goal or objective as a prime motivator.

Executives and managers are not all at equal risk of depression. While the average risk may be 10 percent or so for depression among managers and executives, for those in the high-technology sector of the economy, the risk is greater. The risk varies also by one's career and life stage. Therefore, executives and managers in the middle years are at heightened risk of depression, as are those executives and managers just following retirement.

Although the most common symptom of depression is melancholy, it is often accompanied by physical symptoms. These include eating and sleeping disorders as well as loss of interest in sex. In some cases indigestion, constipation, and headaches may be symptoms of depression. Finally, suicidal attempts are an extreme symptom. This was the case for US Chief of Naval Operations Jeremy M. Boorda who committed suicide on Thursday, May 16, 1996 at the age of 56. The triggering event in this sad case appeared to be an investigative reporting of his past combat record and his wearing of combat decorations, which some people questioned.

Anxiety

Anxiety and depression are the most common presenting complaints to family physicians. While anxiety disorders affect about 16 percent of the

American population and about 20 percent of the working population in the United Kingdom, there is not good data to indicate the rate of occurrence of anxiety disorders among executives and managers. Anxiety, like stress, is not necessarily a problem. Anxiety is an appropriate fear-related response when in circumstances which are threatening, dangerous, or highly uncertain. However, anxiety becomes a health problem when it turns into one or another anxiety disorders. Freud was the first to address the problem of anxiety, and there are now seven categories of anxiety disorders, which include acute stress disorder, post-traumatic stress disorder (PTSD), panic disorder, obsessive-compulsive disorder, social phobia, agoraphobia, and generalized anxiety disorder.

> Freud was the first to address the problem of anxiety, and there are now seven categories of anxiety disorders, which include acute stress disorder, post-traumatic stress disorder (PTSD), panic disorder, obsessive-compulsive disorder, social phobia, agoraphobia, and generalized anxiety disorder.

Both acute stress disorder and PTSD follow some traumatic or catastrophic event, such as a workplace fatality. Acute stress disorder is a characteristic pattern of anxiety, dissociation, and other symptoms that occur during or immediately after a traumatic event. For example, the chairman of Luby's Cafeterias most likely experienced acute stress disorder upon learning of the suicide of the company's CEO in 1998. He ultimately found it necessary to resign his position with the company. The symptoms last at least two days and often resolve within one month, with or without treatment. However, acute stress disorder may also evolve into depression, PTSD, or one of several other chronic conditions.

In contrast to acute stress disorder, PTSD symptoms last for more than one month. Early research with PTSD focused on military combat veterans, such as the former senator Bob Kerry, who were subject to war traumas, and on those subject to natural disasters. However, increasing attention is being given to executives, managers, and professionals subject to industrial accidents, such as occurred for Union Carbide in Bhopal India, and to workplace violence, such as occurred at the law firm of Petit & Martin in San Francisco (France, Arndt, 2001). While homicide and suicide clearly qualify as workplace traumatic events, so to a lesser extent do layoffs and relocations.

Panic disorder is characterized by periodic panic attacks with a range of symptoms, such as palpitations, sweating, trembling, shortness of breath, and other acute symptoms. There may be predictable triggers for panic attacks for some executives or managers. One such trigger may be public speaking events, or flying. Panic disorder is very treatable, especially if it is limited to known trigger events.

Howard Hughes is one well-known executive with notable anxiety disorders, which ultimately led him to a highly reclusive, secretive life. The evidence seems to suggest a combination of obsessive–compulsive disorder, social phobia, and agoraphobia. While all of these anxiety disorders are highly treatable, leading to a fuller and richer life, left untreated they are each and together very debilitating because of the limitations that they place upon an executive's or manager's full range of functions and activities. While debilitating, the anxiety disorders do not tend to be immediately life threatening in the way undiagnosed and untreated depression can be when it places its victim at risk of suicide or cardiovascular disease.

Physical inactivity

Long hours, frequent travel, evening meetings, community responsibilities, and family commitments all conspire against a habit of regular physical exercise. And if the habit did not develop early in life, it is even more difficult to begin in adulthood. Yet according to the World Health Organization, lack of activity contributes to more than 2 million deaths per year worldwide. Physical inactivity is associated with premature death from coronary heart disease, diabetes, and certain cancers. It is also associated with greater disability from arthritis, increase risk of falls among older populations, and a myriad of other adverse affects on health and well-being. Physiologically, the pattern of ill-effects associated with physical inactivity look remarkably like the pattern of effects associated with aging.

Substantial health benefits are best achieved with regular, sustained physical activity – defined as five or more times per week for 30 minutes or more per occasion. Based on this definition, only about one in four men and only one in five women in the United States are physically active.

In the United Kingdom, using the same definition as in the United States, over one-third of men and one-quarter of women engage in recommended amounts of moderate to strenuous physical activity (US Department of Health and Human Services, 1996). Overall within the EU countries, one-third of adults have no leisure-time physical activity in a typical week. Almost half of the EU population spend two to six hours per day sitting at work and one-fifth spend six hours or more sitting (British Heart Foundation, 2002). Among men in the US, there is relatively little variation in the percentage who are physically active between those 30 to 44 years of age and those over 65 years of age. However, the pattern of physical activity seems to change substantially with age. In the 1991 National Health Interview Survey, compared to men over age 65, men age 30 to 44 were nearly twice as likely to bicycle (18 percent versus 10 percent) and ten times more likely to jog or run (14 percent versus 1.4 percent).

One survey of executives from the top 3,000 US companies found that two-thirds of executives exercised at least three times weekly, suggesting a level of fitness above average for the United States (British Heart Foundation, 2000). Data from the United Kingdom, however, indicates that half of men working in unskilled manual employment meet the above recommended levels of regular exercise, compared with less than one-third in professional jobs. Similarly, physical activity is greatest among people with mid-range household incomes and lowest at the extremes of high and low income (Neck, Cooper, 2000).

Unhealthy eating and excess weight

It has been observed wryly, but perhaps accurately, that the average body weight of CEOs declined over the 1990s. This is not just because there are more women CEOs, but because many CEOs – men and women – have gotten the message that physical health matters, and that weight control is an important part of physical health.

Nevertheless, in 1999, an estimated 61 percent of American were overweight or obese, making the US the weightiest major society in history. In both Europe and the United States, overweight and obesity have doubled since 1980 (British Heart Foundation, 2000), accounting for about 300,000 excess deaths per year in the US alone, and making it second only to cigarette smoking as a preventable cause of death. Excess deaths from overweight and obesity are due primarily to heart disease and stroke resulting from increases in hypertension, lipid disorders, and diabetes. Overweight and obesity also lead to worsening of arthritis, sleep disturbances, and skin disorders. In 2000, direct and indirect costs of overweight and obesity in the United States were estimated at $117 billion. In Europe, the health impact of increasing overweight and obesity is having a significant impact on health care costs (US Department of Health and Human Services, 2001). Though there remains some debate, current evidence indicates that genetic factors account for only about one-third of variations in body weight. Some medications for depression, anxiety, and other conditions may contribute to weight gain. But for most people excess body fat results from the simple imbalance between diet and activity. Like a bank account, if deposits (calorie intake) are greater than withdrawals (calorie consumption), the balance goes up.

Tobacco, alcohol, and drug abuse

Substance abuse is the final major health problem for which executives and managers are at risk. Substance abuse includes legal substances and prescription drugs as well as those that are illegal. Tobacco, alcohol, and drug abuse pose major health risks for executives and managers. Substance abuse can be a very hidden and insidious health-risk factor for at least two reasons. First, there are the social, cultural, and religious taboos that accompany the use of tobacco, alcohol, and drugs. These taboos may lead an executive or manager to engage in substance use in clandestine ways that are hard to diagnose and, therefore, to treat in their early stages. Second, many drugs and substances, while toxic in nature are also therapeutic in medicinal doses. Hence, these can serve as double-edged swords that may aid health and healing when used appropriately, while also presenting serious health consequences when improperly managed.

Tobacco use and abuse may be the most visible of the health threats for executives and managers. In addition to its contribution to heart disease and stroke, tobacco use is a significant predictor of a wide range of cancers. Former chairman and CEO Roberto Goizueta of Coca-Cola was well known for smoking cigars. Subsequent to his development of cancer and his premature death, the company entered several years of struggle and turmoil in the leadership of the firm. No one can know if Mr Goizueta might have been able to play a positive role in helping to avert or better manage some of the challenges of this period by relying on his vast experience in leading Coke, had he survived.

Health consequences –
the executive heart attack

The executive risks described above have a direct and powerful influence on physical health, sense of well-being, and productivity, with the most powerful, and lethal, effects being from heart attacks, strokes and other forms of cardiovascular disease. Cardiovascular disease has been the leading cause of death in the United States, Europe and other parts of the industrialized world for 100 years. The cardiovascular system is centrally implicated in the stress response and secondarily implicated in the anxiety disorders. Undiagnosed and untreated heart disease can be deadly, as in the case of TI's Jerry Junkins. Contrary to stereotypes of high-pressure CEOs, however, executives and managers at the second or third tier of the organization may be at greater risk of cardiovascular problems than the chairmen and CEOs who have achieved the success and achievement for which they strove.

> Many of the known risk factors can be managed, although at least three of the major risk factors for heart disease cannot be altered. These three are age, male sex, and heredity, including family history and race.

While cardiovascular disease is the number-one killer, it may also be the best-profiled executive health problem in terms of known risk factors. Many of the known risk factors can be managed, although at least three of the major risk factors for heart disease cannot be altered. These three are age, male sex, and heredity, including family history and race. Of those who die of heart disease, 80 percent are aged 65 or older, and men are at greater risk than are women. In addition, a family history of heart disease or inclusion in a high-risk racial group predisposes one to cardiovascular problems. Executives and managers, however, can take actions that significantly lower their risk of experiencing heart disease.

Among the known risk factors, there are at least six which executives can manage directly: tobacco smoke, high blood cholesterol, high blood pressure, physical inactivity, obesity and overweight, and diabetes mellitus. Tobacco use, lack of physical activity, and improper diet account for up to 80 percent of premature coronary heart disease, according to the World Health Organization. Smoking alone increases the risk of cardiovascular problems by two to four times in addition to its contribution to other health problems. (One limitation in the research that has identified these known risk factors is the small sample of women who have been included in any of the studies.) Virtually all of these manageable risk factors are related to lifestyle choices and behaviors over which executives and managers have control. The effects of lifestyle and behavior choices on cardiac function have become increasingly well understood over the past several decades.

One factor that has received renewed attention over the past decade is the impact of emotions on cardiovascular health. The early research of Walter B. Cannon brought attention to the impact of emotions related to pain, hunger, fear, and rage on the nervous and cardiovascular systems in the body. Redford Williams more recently (1993) has found that the emotion of anger is lethal, and can kill. Williams's newer research has shown that emotional well-being has positive effects on cardiovascular health while, alternatively, a negative emotional life has ill effects on cardiovascular health. This may be exemplified in the case of Dwight D. Eisenhower who, as president of the United States, was reported to be highly agitated and angry just prior to his heart attack in 1955. His heart attack caused real trauma and concern throughout the country, with very short-term adverse economic impacts.

Health-risk assessment:

Early diagnosis, early warning

Health-risk assessment can lead to early diagnosis and early warning of emerging problems for executives. Early diagnosis is one of the best interventions for preventing serious health problems. The Duke Executive Health Program, chosen by General Motors Corporation as a center of excellence in executive health, has as one of its distinguishing features an emphasis on comprehensive health assessment, using a preventive medicine orientation. Physicians, clinical health psychologists, registered dieticians, and exercise physiologists conduct Duke's four-component health assessment outlined in Table 2.2.

Table 2.2 Executive health assessment

Medical evaluation
- medical history
- laboratory tests

Psychosocial risk-factor screening
- perceived stress
- hostility/cynicism
- depression
- social support

Nutrition assessment
- dietary patterns and lifestyle issues
- three-day food journal

Fitness assessment
- flexibility
- cardiovascular
- strength

Source: Duke Executive Health Program.

- *Medical evaluation.* The first component of the comprehensive assessment is the medical evaluation, which begins with a medical history followed by a complete physical exam and set of laboratory tests. Supplementary diagnostic procedures may include a flexible sigmoidoscopy for colon cancer and other abnormalities of the lower large intestine, homocysteine test for coronary artery disease, eye examination, and HIV test. For women executives, additional services include mammography, gynecological examination, pap smear, quantitative digital radiography to test bone density for osteoporosis, and abdominal/pelvic ultrasound.

- *Psychosocial risk factor screening.* The second component is the psychosocial screening for the health risk factors noted in Table 2.2. Stress, hostility, depression, and the lack of social support are all known health-risk factors, and may be underassessed in executives. Depression is a major risk factor for suicide, as seen in the case of Admiral Boorda.

- *Nutrition assessment.* The third component is a nutrition assessment that includes a review of typical dietary patterns of the executive, as well as executive lifestyle issues that affect food choices. Diet has been demonstrated to play a role in robust health and in a wide range of health disorders, from obesity to cardiovascular disease. This is done under the supervision of a registered dietician and aimed at fitting health nutrition into an executive's active lifestyle.

● *Fitness assessment.* The fourth component is the fitness assessment along the three dimensions listed in Table 2.2. An exercise physiologist can use the assessment as the basis for creating a detailed prescription outlining the frequency, duration, and intensity of an executive's fitness activities. A customized plan with training recommendations is an executive's blueprint for action.

Preventive health management

In Chapter 1 we described the vice-grip in which many executives find themselves, and raised the question as to whether executives are in the midst of a job stress epidemic. Prevention is the appropriate response, epidemic or not. The executive health problems discussed in this chapter are not inevitable. There is a wide range of preventive health management practices we discuss throughout the book which strengthen an executive against these risks and potential problems. In addition, quick response to early warning signs and accurate early diagnosis are essential ingredients in the practice of preventive medicine and preventive health maintenance. These are important not only for the executive's health but for the collective well-being of the organization.

Organizational consequences of executive health

Executive health is not simply a personal issue; it has collective consequences for all members of any organization who depend upon the strength, experience, skills, and insights of its leaders. The temporary or permanent loss of an executive, especially a chief executive, can have very adverse consequences for the whole organization. Conversely, one strong, healthy executive in a key organizational position can serve as a primary prevention agent for tens, hundreds, and even thousands of employees who serve under his or her wing. Therefore, the interests of the organization as well as its individual executives are served well by the preventive health management of its executive cadre.

Chapter 2 in a nutshell

1. Executive stress can lead to enhanced performance and high achievement if it is well managed and not excessive or unrelenting.

2. Executives are vulnerable to the same medical, psychological, and behavioral health problems and disorders which may afflict any person.

3. Workaholism, burnout, depression, and anxiety are central psychological health risks for executives at work.

4. Physical inactivity, unhealthy eating habits, and substance abuse (including smoking) are key risk factors which contribute to heart attacks and other major health consequences.

5. Health risk assessments and preventive health management are key weapons for executives in combating these problems and disorders.

3

The loneliness of command

People ask the difference between a leader and a boss . . . The leader works in the open, and the boss in covert. The leader leads, and the boss drives.

Theodore Roosevelt (1858–1919), US Republican (later Progressive) politician, president. Speech, October 24, 1910, Binghamton, NY

The penalty of leadership is loneliness.

H. Wheeler Robinson, Baptist scholar and past-president of the Society for Old Testament Study

For most people who enter management positions, the ultimate goal is to continue climbing the corporate ladder and to achieve a top executive position. Those who aspire to these goals see the external side of executive positions. They see the power, glamour, and prestige of such jobs, but they usually miss the other side of such high-level and highly visible positions. Few executives allow even their closest subordinates to see the lonelier side of an executive position.

Executives at or near the top of an organization often experience feelings of emotional isolation or loneliness. Top leadership positions, by design, separate the person from others, leaving them with no peers inside the organization. They have little or no support in dealing with the natural need for affiliation and companionship. Executives are often left with no one they can bounce ideas on and elicit feedback from. They are faced with isolation not only from others but also from the feedback necessary to make the best decisions.

While many executives function in this imposed isolation, understanding the causes and the potential risks of isolation is extremely important. In this chapter, we will offer insight into the causes of isolation, discuss the outcomes to the executive and his or her organizations, and finally suggest some preventive measures to help the executive and the organization flourish.

Causes of isolation

In addition to the very nature of the job – forcing the isolation of the leader – aspects of the organization and culture, as well as personality traits of the individual, may lead to isolation and loneliness for executives. From an organizational perspective, the vertical nature of most hierarchies forces those at higher levels to be increasingly separated from those at lower levels. With each move up the ladder, the individual is disconnected from more of his or her friends and peers. The degree of interaction the individual once shared with these peers may now be seen as excessive fraternization with subordinates.

Cultural values are another component that can contribute to the isolation of leaders. Most western cultures place great value on independence. Our culture admires people who are willing to take on battles, especially those who are willing to face those challenges alone. Even in the workplace, employees tend to idealize their leaders. Organization members often, whether consciously or unconsciously, see their leaders as infallible and possessing some degree of "magical" powers (Kets de Vries, 1994). This almost mystical vision of the executive puts great pressure on the executive to hide all weaknesses.

Finally, two elements of personality can add to the problems of isolation and loneliness that many executives experience. The first is counterdependence. Counterdependence is one of the dysfunctional outcomes when a child does not develop strong healthy attachments during his or her developmental years. When a child "attaches" to his or her parents, especially during times of threat or crisis, the parents are there to support and sustain the child and to provide whatever is needed; consequently, the child grows up healthy and secure and becomes a self-reliant adult. However, when the child attaches to figures that are not reliable or consistently there for support, the child can develop dysfunctional strategies for achieving a sense of security during those times of danger. One of those strategies is counterdependence, which consists of avoiding or denying one's needs in times of threat or danger. It represents an individual's attempt to achieve self-sufficiency in relation to others by distancing oneself from others. In other words, it allows the individual who has never been able to rely on others in time of need to find comfort by ignoring the need for the support of others. People who are counterdependent become isolated and lonely at precisely those times when it is least appropriate to be so. This personality trait, if present in the executive, will only exacerbate the inherent loneliness of the job.

The second personality trait is interpersonal defensiveness. Again, this is a dispositional factor that will enhance the natural tendencies toward isolation already discussed. Interpersonal defensiveness always leads the individual to establish barriers between him or herself and others, to create distance in relationships, and to develop a wide range of communication dysfunctions. In addition, the individual may display active defensiveness, embodied by the attitude that one's self is always right and others are always wrong. Another type of defensiveness is more passive, expressed in an attitude of "excuse me for living." Either form leads to the same outcome of increasing the problem of isolation and loneliness, as we will see in the following examples.

Semon "Bunkie" Knudsen

Sometimes the isolation of command is more understandable, for instance, when an outsider is brought into an organization to accept the leadership position. One memorable example of a successful outsider who failed after having been hired to run a different organization was Semon "Bunkie" Knudsen (Iacocca, 1984). Bunkie Knudsen was the wonder boy of the 1960s automobile industry in Detroit. He was the son of William Knudsen, the Danish immigrant who became the head of Chevrolet in the 1920s. Bunkie had, however, earned recognition in his own right. At the age of 44, Bunkie was made head of the Pontiac Division of General Motors (GM), the youngest division head in GM's history.

In 1968, Henry Ford II managed to lure Knudsen away from GM for a mere $600,000 a year, the same salary Ford was receiving at the time.

Knudsen took over as president of Ford in the late winter of 1968. He managed to remain there for only 19 months. What could happen in such a short span of time to reduce the wonder boy of Detroit to a dismal failure? One of the best answers to that question is the isolation Knudsen experienced during that time.

No bigger rivalry existed in Detroit, then or now, than the one between GM and Ford. Bunkie Knudsen walked into Ford not only as an outsider but also, in the minds of many at Ford, as the competition. The people in the top positions at Ford were resentful of being asked to work for someone from GM. In addition, they never believed that the GM system of management would work at Ford, nor did they go out of their way to help Knudsen understand this. They sat back and watched and waited for him to fail, and in reality their behavior ensured it.

Knudsen brought with him the mindset of GM. From Henry Ford's perspective, this would marry the best of the two organizations. But the two cultures did not mix well. Knudsen never worked within the system that was established at Ford. He bypassed lines of authority in his attempts to lead the company, and in the process he alienated a lot of people, including Henry Ford. The end of Bunkie Knudsen's career at Ford has forever been memorialized in the phrase that soon became famous throughout Ford: "Henry Ford [I] once said that history is bunk. But today Bunkie is history (Higgins, 2001)."

As described in the story of Bunkie Knudsen, isolation at the top of an organization can be difficult. But a story such as Knudsen's seems easier to understand given his lack of knowledge and understanding of the organization, culture, and people at Ford. Knudsen's case is the classic example of the isolating effects of the hierarchical nature of an organization and the lack of peer relationships caused by being an outsider. Little in this story demonstrates the impact that the executive's psychology may have on his or her behavior. The case of John Curtis Jr offers a much more disturbing example of how personality may play a deadly role in taking the isolation and loneliness of the executive's life to much more serious levels than just the loss of a job (*Newsweek*, March 31, 1997).

John Curtis Jr

From every outward appearance, John Curtis was the epitome of the American success story. Before the age of 50, he had just been named CEO of a very successful chain of cafeterias. The year before attaining the CEO position, he had earned $358,000 in compensation as president. He was married to his grade-school sweetheart and was the father of three children. No one appears to have foreseen what was to be a single horrifying act by a man who seemingly had everything going for him.

Curtis graduated, with honors, from Texas Tech University in 1969. Soon after graduation, he married the girl who fell in love with him in the sixth grade, Kathie. Together, they had three children, of whom the older two followed in their father's footsteps, becoming Certified Public Accountants. Curtis was also a trustee in his evangelical church and was known as someone ready and willing to assist anyone in need.

Curtis joined the Luby's organization in 1979. Rising through the ranks at Luby's, he attained the chief financial officer position in 1988. Eight years later, he was promoted to president. He reached the top spot, chief executive officer, in January 1997. Members of the Luby's organization and his family described Curtis in very positive terms. He was known as a very dedicated man and a perfectionist. His predecessor, Ralph Erben, said that Curtis had "a real sense of dignity." His wife claimed, "He loved me well, and his children. He was a good man, a Godly man" (*Houston Chronicle*, March 15, 1997). Finally, observers say that Curtis seemed excited about the expansion plans of the Luby's restaurants, in addition to a joint venture with a Corpus Christie seafood restaurant concept called Water Street, Inc.

With everything looking so good, everyone seems baffled by what happened next. On March 14, 1997, John Curtis checked into a Motel 6, and sometime that night he took his own life. The next morning his wife discovered a suicide note he had left for her. His body was found that same morning by the police in the motel room lying in a pool of blood. The description of his suicide is just as puzzling as the event itself. It was reported that using a kitchen knife, he first tried to die by hacking his left wrist and then his upper abdomen. Finally, he thrust the knife into his neck three times, completing the act by severing the right jugular vein.

In the wake of the devastating news, people who knew him best were shocked. No one, either at Luby's or his family, could explain what had happened to their beloved leader. His wife stated at his memorial service: "I have no doubt that some oppressive darkness overtook his mind." His son Daniel stated: "There were no extenuating circumstances. I don't think he could handle the pressure of being a CEO." Even the man who hand-picked Curtis to succeed him as CEO had no idea of the difficulties facing him. Mr Erben was as shocked as anyone when he heard the news.

In the investigation following his death, it appears that Curtis was troubled over the company's performance. His wife reportedly told the police that possible store closings and related workforce layoffs were affecting her husband's sleep habits. Lastly, there was also a slight decline in Luby's profit margin that Curtis was scheduled to discuss at the next day's meeting with the company's directors. Whatever it was, it appears that Curtis could not bear to deal with the situation in a constructive manner.

Outcomes of isolation

Behavioral outcomes

Ambitious executives spend their careers climbing to the top positions in organizations. Regardless of the personal cost, they are ready and willing to pay it. If the organization favors a strong work ethic, these go-getters will put in more hours than anyone else. They will be the first to arrive at the office and the last to leave at night. If the organization favors aggressiveness, these individuals will display aggressiveness enough to frighten most people. In the game of office politics, these folks excel. No price is too high on the road to the CEO position.

> Ambitious executives spend their careers climbing to the top positions in organizations. Regardless of the personal cost, they are ready and willing to pay it.

Networking and building relationships are a very important aspect of the ambitious executive's makeup. On the way to the top, he or she realizes that certain relationships are critical to winning the top spot. For instance, mentor relationships are very important. Such a relationship enables the aspiring leader to steer clear of obstacles and gain valuable insights into company decisions and actions.

Few top executives are truly prepared for the changes that occur once they reach their ultimate career goal. On the way to the top, the aspiring leader will generally engage in actions that propel him or her into the fast track. For instance, key relationships with the "right people" will be established: the right mentor, the right boss, and the right peers. The aspiring executive will join the right clubs, read the accepted magazines and newspapers, and engage in the popular sports. Another important aspect of the journey to the top is the amount and types of restraints with which the aspiring leader has to contend. The most obvious restraint comes from having a superior. Even the most aggressive leader doesn't want to offend his superior, which might retard his progress. Likewise, the aspiring leader's peers provide some restraint on his or her actions. Specifically, being challenged, ridiculed, or gossiped about can have a devastating effect on the aspiring leader.

It is all too common for leaders to have strong feelings of loneliness and being disconnected from the rest of the organization. It is also common for leaders to engage in self-defeating behaviors. If not caught in time, such behaviors can have negative effects on subordinates, the health of the organization, and the career of the top executive.

For instance, the restraints that kept the aspiring leader in check on the way to the top spot are suddenly removed. The relationships that were important to achieving success may no longer carry the same meaning. The change may come from subordinates who now see the leader as different and apart from them. The subordinates may them- selves be restrained from communicating in an open and frank way. Mentor relationships may cease now that the leader has attained the prized position. The leader may not value the advice he or she once sought. Relationships with superiors dissolve when the executive becomes the superior. Unless a functioning and competent board exerts appropriate influence, the leader may unconsciously believe that there are no restraints holding him or her from future success.

With the restraints removed, the leader may engage in grandiose proj- ects that may or may not be successful. If the projects are successful, the leader justifies the hero worship given by subordinates. On the other hand, if the projects are failures, the unrestrained leader may be unable to see and hear the warning signs. The leader may also engage in blaming subordinates for the failure. All of these behaviors will cause distress for the subordinates and erosion for the organization.

Depression is another self-defeating behavior in which the leader may engage. When the leader has feelings of isolation and loneliness that go unchecked, depression is a real possibility. As the leader sinks deeper into depression, he or she may feel more and more lonely and isolated. This may lead to irrational decisions and behaviors that lead in turn to alienating subordinates and customers. The people that once helped the executive on the way to the top are now seen as untrustworthy or, at the least, having a different agenda than the leader. Depression may also lead to additional self-defeating behaviors such as alcoholism, drug use, or other means of escape. These addictions may culminate in the eventual destruction of the leader's career.

Sometimes, leaders engage in sabotaging their own success due to sub-conscious feelings of anxiety and guilt. They may be anxious about being successful in their new position. They may feel guilt about how they achieved the top spot even if they truly deserve it. They may also feel that they have betrayed those people who have not achieved the same success.

Transference is also a potential problem for the leader. Employees may transfer prior feelings about authority figures onto the leader. They may "idealize" the leader in order to replicate feelings of safety and secu-rity that they had experienced with early authority figures. This idealizing may cause the leader to get an inflated ego. The employees may seek to win the leader's favor and may become "yes men."

On the negative side, employees may blame their leaders for failing to live up to their idealized expectations. This can lead to employees moving from admiration to hostility. The leader is then blamed as responsible for the company's problems. If the leader starts to feel this blame and to feel unjustly prosecuted, he or she may retaliate against the employees. This could cause much fear and anxiety throughout the company.

J. Clifford Baxter

Sometimes the blame and responsibility placed on executives becomes overwhelming for them. And there are times when the executive per-sonally accepts more of the blame than even the employees deem appropriate for that individual. One recent situation that seems to

exemplify this situation is J. Clifford "Cliff" Baxter of Enron Corporation. In late 2001, Enron collapsed into bankruptcy, leaving many creditors, shareholders and employees penniless. The impending collapse
of the corporate giant had been obvious to the executives of Enron for
several months; however, they remained
quiet about their financial problems to all
stakeholders. All the while, top executives
were cashing in their stock and walking
away with an estimated $1.1 billion
between October 1998 and November
2001 (www.msnbc.com/news).

Cliff Baxter was among the 29 past and
current executives and board members
named as defendants in a federal lawsuit
filed in January 2002. The plaintiffs
claimed that Baxter had sold 577,436 shares of Enron stock for $35.2
million. Unable or unwilling to face these charges, Baxter took his own
life on January 25, 2002. Police in the Houston, Texas, suburb of Sugar-
land found Baxter in his car dead from a self-inflicted gunshot wound
to the head. Baxter was only 43 years old at the time of his death.

> Sometimes the blame and responsibility placed on executives becomes overwhelming for them. And there are times when the executive personally accepts more of the blame than even the employees deem appropriate for that individual.

While most employees, stakeholders, and the public in general
placed the blame for the Enron collapse on the leaders of the corporation, Cliff Baxter was held by most as to be one of the few executives
who attempted to stop the deception of stakeholders as early as the
spring of 2001. Baxter resigned from Enron in May 2001, stating that
he wanted to spend more time with his family. Many believe, however,
that the resignation was a direct result of the financial practices that
Enron executives were using to keep hundreds of millions of dollars
in debt off Enron's books.

Physiological outcomes

One of the outcomes of the isolation of the leader is that he or she is
often left without complete or accurate knowledge of the organization
and its members. This lack of information may further enhance the feelings of loneliness by leaving the executive out of the simplest of conver-
sations. The effects of isolation and feelings of loneliness are much more

devastating than is commonly understood. The work of James Lynch (2000) clearly demonstrates this point. Beginning in the 1960s, Lynch has researched large groups of people who end up in hospitals due to congestive heart failure. His findings have been groundbreaking on the effects of emotional isolation.

One of the most important findings is that people are frequently unaware of the effects that isolation and loneliness have on their health. For instance, while discussing hurtful experiences, the patient's heart was exhibiting symptoms that could have led to the person having another heart attack. Many times in his interviews, Lynch, would interrupt the patient recalling the hurtful experience, ask them to calm down, and begin to breathe slowly and deeply. When Lynch then asked if the patient felt the effects being displayed on the blood pressure monitor, the patient frequently said "no." In other words, their bodies were displaying great stress, but the patient was totally unaware of the condition.

While it may be easy simply to prescribe more human contact as an antidote for this isolation and loneliness, Lynch discovered that it is not that simple. For instance, a person can be in a packed stadium and still feel isolated and alone. The real test of eradicating loneliness is for the lonely person to experience real human communication and contact with just one other person.

Lynch sums up his approach to treating patients who have experienced congestive heart failure as the "physiology of inclusion." This "physiology of inclusion" is a state of harmony between the person and the world in which they live. This is in contrast to the "physiology of exclusion," which describes how a person may exist in an endless state of self-preservation in which one is in competition with the world for one's very survival. This is also known as the classic fight-or-flight mode, which causes a perpetual state of isolation and loneliness.

Preventive measures for executives

Although the risk that managers and executives face from isolation and the loneliness that may accompany it are significant, there are several things an individual can do to prevent negative outcomes and health problems. In this section of the chapter, we will cover several techniques for coping with the problem. These techniques include executive coaching, external peer support, confidants and journal writing.

Executive coaching

One of the most effective and popular methods of dealing with the lack of effective feedback from within an organization is executive coaching. Executive coaches offer executives, managers, and business owners a safe, confidential forum for expressing ideas, challenges and concerns. Coaches provide sounding boards and offer the critical feedback that an executive's life often lacks once peers are no longer peers but subordinates.

Coaches provide managers and executives with an individual who has no personal stake in the process other than helping the client with his or her ideas and concerns. The coach is not just a confidant to whom the executive can freely speak, but he or she is usually also someone who is knowledgeable about the organization, the industry and/or the psychological aspects of counseling the individual. In some cases a coach may be more beneficial than a personal confidant, because the coach can be more emotionally removed and thus deal with the executive's issues from a more objective perspective.

Many managers and executives have experienced coaching in the form of mentoring from more experienced executives. While mentoring is an extremely effective way to help develop and grow managers and executives, as the individual rises through the organization there are fewer and fewer mentors to whom the person may turn. As the individual reaches the very top levels of the organization, he or she is left without more experienced mentors and must often turn to external sources to provide this necessary function.

Peer support

As mentioned throughout this chapter, finding peers at the upper levels of an organization is often difficult, if not impossible, for most people. While some choose to turn to executive coaches, others choose the route of finding peers outside the organization. If a person is fortunate, they may have friends in other non-competitive organizations who hold similar positions with whom they may confide. However, for many people this person does not currently exist in their lives. One solution to this problem is to join organizations that might afford the opportunity to meet others.

One such organization is the Young Presidents' Organization (YPO: www.ypo.org). Founded in 1950 by Ray Hickok, the YPO first came into existence to help young men who found themselves leading organizations at a very young age and to provide them with the experience necessary to feel comfortable moving forward on their own. Today YPO is an international organization offering both men and women an opportunity to learn from each other and to share experiences.

The mission of YPO is to "create better leaders through education and idea exchange worldwide." Through membership, individuals can tap into unlimited sources of personal experiences and ideas to help them address the concerns and problems they currently face. Membership in YPO or other similar organizations can play a significant role in replacing the peer support lost by the executive.

Confidants

In some cases, leaders and executives feel they have plenty of knowledge and support for the continued success of their organization and their personal performance. These executives' needs tend to be more on the personal side. They need someone to whom they can confide their emotions, someone who will listen to them and understand their most intimate and private fears and concerns. To solve this need, many executives turn to their spouses.

Managers and executives who are lucky enough to have a well-established relationship with a spouse or partner may have the greatest asset possible to address this need. History offers several examples of executives who relied on the personal support and feedback of trusted spouses. One case is that of Lee Iacocca, who had a history of support from his wife of 37 years, Mary. While we do not have written documentation of this relationship, as we do in some of the following cases, we have an indirect indicator of that support in Iacocca's reaction to Mary's death in 1983 (Romano, 1985). With his support system gone, Iacocca seemed to lose his grounding. In the next 11 years, he married and divorced twice. He struggled to find in someone else the support system he had had in Mary.

Another case of a chief executive with strong spousal support is President John Adams, who lived in a different city than his wife Abigail for a good deal of their marriage. This long-distance relationship is richly detailed in the correspondence between the two. Abigail's love, support, and understanding were clearly a benefit and source of strength for Adams. Probably the most documented case of spousal support, however, is that between Winston and Clementine Churchill. In her book, *Winston and Clementine: The Personal Letters of the Churchills*, Mary Soames offers us a look into the private world of her parents. The love and intimacy that the Churchills shared is evident. The support that this relationship offered Winston as he faced the pressures of his office during World War II may have been immeasurable.

Journal writing

One of the most interesting and simplest methods of dealing with the effects of isolation can be found in journal writing. James Pennebaker has done extensive research on the effects of journal writing on people who have experienced trauma. The remarkable outcomes experienced by his research subjects are nothing short of amazing.

For instance, writing about events that trouble us helps us resolve unfinished business. Top executives tend to get bombarded with issues all day long. Frequently, it is difficult to solve or bring closure to every issue that causes them to spend countless hours thinking about their businesses. This also contributes to sleeplessness and the negative effects associated with it.

Writing forces the top executive to stop thinking about the multitude of outstanding issues, and refocuses his mind on just one issue. By making a conscious effort to communicate clearly on paper, or on the computer, the executive must begin the process of thinking clearly and logically and to organize his thoughts so that his writing can be understood and have meaning. Simply put, the writing process forces us to structure and organize our thoughts into coherent sentences.

Pennebaker discovered that unresolved issues tend to reside in the forefront of a person's thought processes. Only completed issues can be stored away freely and forgotten, thereby allowing us to move on to other thought processes.

Another very positive aspect to writing is that it promotes self-understanding. It helps us discover meaning in difficult situations. There are many times when top executives are dealing with very complex and gray issues that have no right or wrong answers. Many times in decision-making, the top executive knows that whatever decision he or she makes, someone will benefit and someone will be disadvantaged. This often leaves many executives looking for meaning behind their decision-making so that they believe they have done the "right" thing.

Writing has also been shown to be very therapeutic for people who have to deal with defeat. Regardless of how successful a company is, or a top executive is, there will be times when a loss will occur. Top executives are, by nature, very competitive. They engage in competition all the time. The simple fact is that no one wins all of the time. The use of writing has shown that it can help people bounce back quickly from defeat.

When people write about defeats, they can become more detached from the situation. That is, they can begin to view the situation objectively and to make more rational observations regarding it. One of the best discoveries made about the effect of the writing process is that emotional responses are less extreme. This too contributes to a more objective interpretation of the traumatic event. These benefits all lead the top executive toward resolving issues and freeing the mind to work on new events.

The bottom line on writing is that it has shown again and again that it can improve a person's health and job performance. Used as a daily habit, it can additionally be used to help the top executive to bring closure to outstanding and unresolved issues. Then the top executive can face each day ready to take on new challenges and deal with them effectively.

Conclusion

While little to nothing can be done about the nature of the executive position and the isolation and loneliness that accompanies it, managers and executives can become aware of the risks and potential outcomes that accompany this problem. Each in his or her own way can address this problem by seeking out the type of support that is most beneficial. But the problem must be addressed in some fashion, or disastrous outcomes may result, for both the executive and his or her organization.

Chapter 3 in a nutshell

1. Executives and managers should expect to experience a certain level of isolation and feelings of loneliness as they move to higher levels in the organization.

2. There are cultural, organizational and personal causes for this loneliness.

3. Executives who experience this isolation and loneliness are at risk of both behavioral and psychological problems.

4. Executive coaching, peer support, confidants and journal writing are all techniques for coping with the isolation and loneliness of command.

4

Work demands and travel

In order that people may be happy in their work, these three things are needed: they must be fit for it, they must not do too much of it, and they must have a sense of success in it.

John Ruskin, British social reformer,
at the beginning of the Industrial Revolution, 1851

Balancing the demands of work and business travel with one's relationships with family and loved ones has never been an easy task, and this challenge may be greatest for senior managers and executives who work 60 to 100 hours per week. Excessive workloads, long hours, business travel demands, and the like are undermining the quality of working life for many executives. These pressures not only present risk factors for executives' physical and psychological health, but they also lead to "downshifting" and turnover among key executives. For example, in the United Kingdom the CEO of one of Britain's largest insurers, Danny O'Neil, decided to give up his job at the age of 41 because of the pressures of constant travel and poor balance between his work and his personal life. He told the national press in January 2002 that the crunch came when his 18-year-old daughter left for university, and he realized he hadn't spent the time that he would have liked either with her or with his nine-year-old triplets. He was reported as saying, "I decided on a change in the balance between my work and personal life."

During the same week in January 2002, a top civil servant, who was offered a job as permanent secretary in the British government's Department of International Development, would only take the job if he could leave at 5.30 pm every day to spend time with his young family. This job would normally be a 70-hour-per-week job with loads of unsocial hours (that is, working beyond one's normal, established working hours). But the minister in charge accepted that the work/personal life balance was extremely important, acknowledging the need for better balance, and offering him the job on those grounds. In this chapter we examine those work demands and aspects of business travel that contribute to health risks for executives and may lead either to the kind of limit-setting demanded by the permanent secretary or to resignations such as that of Danny O'Neil.

Sources of stress and pressure at work

While Herb Kelleher has become famous as the funny, creative leader and chief hijackster of Southwest Airlines, the public image belies the serious stress and pressure he experienced at the outset of building the airline in the late 1960s. Kelleher was one of the founders of Air Southwest Company, incorporated in 1967 and certified by the Texas Aeronautics Commission in 1968. However, for the next three years a legal war raged across America before what became Southwest Airlines was able to get its first plane off the ground. Three other airlines (Braniff, Trans Texas, and Continental) fought Kelleher and his airline through the state and federal court systems, including return engagement to the Texas Supreme Court and the United States Supreme Court. The legal battles were grueling, yet Kelleher and Southwest were the final victors. Of the three early opponents of Southwest Airlines, only Continental remains in service. Southwest Airlines was the only major US carrier to not lay off employees as a result of September 11.

While difficult and challenging, litigation is sometimes a necessary evil (or good) in an executive's life. An intense aspect of executive work, litigation is one factor intrinsic to the job, and there are at least six other major sources of pressure for executives. These seven major sources of pressure are:

- factors intrinsic to the job
- travel
- one's role in the organization
- relationships at work
- career stress and the changing nature of work
- organizational and executive cultures
- home–work pressures.

These major sources of stress and pressure are presented in Figure 4.1.

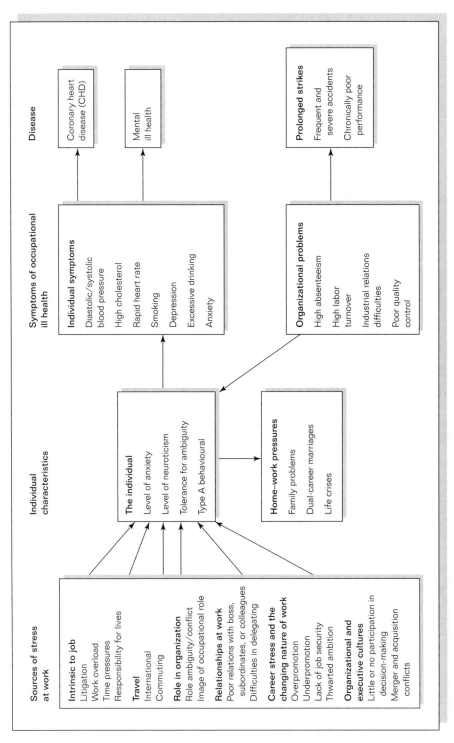

Figure 4.1 A stress and health model (Adapted from Cooper, 1986)

Factors intrinsic to the job

Work overload is a major source of stress for managers and executives. The curvilinear relationship between workload and performance is explained in terms of the Yerkes–Dodson Law we first discussed in Chapter 2 (page 22). This inverted U has health implications, in addition to its performance implications, as shown in Figure 4.2. Work overload may occur because there is too much work to do or because the work is too difficult. Work overload can lead to excessive working hours, further compounding one's stress levels and pressure. Time pressure, such as to meet deadlines, may get confused with work overload but is an independent source of stress. Studies show that stress levels increase as difficult deadlines draw near. We have found high levels of anxiety and depression among British senior tax executives with work overload (Cooper, Roden, 1985).

> Work overload may also occur for the middle manager who has been promoted to a top management job on the grounds of superior work performance but who has no past experience of a strategic role.

Work overload may also occur for the middle manager who has been promoted to a top management job on the grounds of superior work performance but who has no past experience of a strategic role. A good, reliable manager experiences considerable stress because he or she has not yet developed the skills to do the new strategic job. The stress situation may be compounded if the individual has to take disciplinary action against a previous co-worker.

Simply having too much to do in the normal working day leads to overtime working. In addition, the manager who struggles to do a job that is too difficult is likely to take more time to finish the task and may need to work extra hours in order to complete the job to a satisfactory standard. A link has been established between the number of hours worked and death from coronary heart disease (Breslow, Buell, 1960). In addition, a study of 100 young coronary patients showed that 25 percent of them had been working at two jobs, and an additional 40 percent had worked for 60 hours or more per week (Russek, Zohmann, 1958).

For the last five years, the Institute of Management in the United Kingdom has been carrying out a Quality of Working Life survey amongst a representative sample of 5,000 managers, from junior management through to chairman level (Worrall, Cooper, 2001). In 2000, over 40 percent of managers consistently worked over 51 hours per week (with

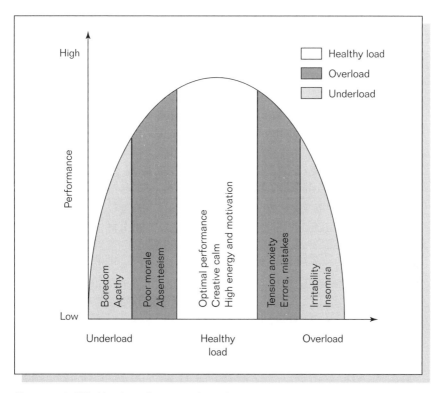

Figure 4.2 Workload–performance hypothesis

nearly 10 percent over 61 hours), with 77 percent working over 41 hours per week. When asked why they work these hours, two out of three say that it is part of the culture of the organization, and 54 percent say it is "expected by my employer" even if they have little to do. The disturbing aspect of this, however, is the impact they say these hours have on their health and relationships, with 65 percent saying it damages their health, 71 percent their community involvement, 59 percent their morale, 59 percent their productivity, 72 percent their relationship with their spouse/partner, and 77 percent their relationship with their children. Interestingly, there is little difference between management levels, with chairmen/CEO reporting similar adverse affects of long hours on their outside relationships, productivity and health.

Travel

Prior to September 11, 2001, extensive air travel was a common charac-teristic of many managerial and executive jobs. Many corporations restrained their executives from commercial air travel immediately following the tragedy, and some companies continue to set clear limits and guidelines. Travel on corporate aircraft is treated somewhat differently, though it is less common for executives. In addition to the frustration, tension and irritation often experienced, the already time-pressured executive is forced to spend even less time in social and family activities. In the aftermath of September 11, the stress-and-hassle factor for air travel, especially for using commercial airports, has increased markedly. While airport security has been an important issue for a long time in many European airports, its importance in US airports has increased significantly. While it has been said that travel broadens the mind, it is equally true that it can blow the mind! Everyday work stress often begins before the executive even reaches the workplace.

Many studies have shown that travel is stress-inducing and impairs job performance. More recently, the World Bank Group's "Stress, the Business Traveler, and Corporate Health" International Health Symposium focused attention on the adverse health effects experienced by executives. In addition, spouses of these traveling executives have significantly more health problems than the spouses of non-traveling executives. Attention has been given to pre-trip, trip, and post-trip demands and stress when examining the health risks associated with travel (DeFrank et al., 2000).

Commuting stress poses a different set of demands on an executive. We found in a study of 120 senior UK executives that the automobile is considered to be the most stressful mode of transportation (Cartwright, Cooper, 1998). In particular, executives report that car journeys lasting in excess of two and a half hours impair their subsequent work performance. Drivers under stress are more likely to take risks, to misjudge the speed of others, or inaccurately to estimate size and distance. Consequently, human factors play a major role in road accidents.

> Drivers under stress are more likely to take risks, to misjudge the speed of others, or inaccurately to estimate size and distance. Consequently, human factors play a major role in road accidents.

Moreover, clear evidence as to the link between stress and accident involvement has emerged from a study of over 100 company-car drivers (Cartwright, Cooper, Barron, 1993). Over a three-year period, the executive drivers who were involved in accidents had significantly higher stress levels than did their accident-free colleagues. The driver's age was not related to accident involvement; however, the executive drivers who exercised time-management skills for stress had fewer accidents than executives who did not exercise these skills. This is because effective time managers allow for contingency time when planning journeys and arranging work schedules, thus reducing time-urgent driving.

Role in the organization

Robert Kahn's classic research (1964) has clearly shown two major causes of organizational stress to be role conflict and ambiguity. More recently there has been a focus on the degree of responsibility for others as a major source of stress associated with an executive's role in the organization.

Role conflict arises for a person at work when the expectations of other people are in conflict. For example, Carly Fiorina experienced significant role conflict as CEO of Hewlett-Packard when the sons of the company's two founders strongly and publicly opposed HP's acquisition of Compaq Inc., a position that was directly in conflict with the majority of her board of directors who supported the acquisition. As in this example, many managers may often feel torn between two groups of people who demand different types of behavior or who believe the job entails different functions. Senior executive positions are fraught with role conflicts when different stakeholders have diametrically opposing expectations of the executive.

Role ambiguity is a second major source of stress for executives and arises when there are confusing, unclear expectations for job performance. This ambiguity may result from a senior executive not laying out a clear understanding of his or her role for a manager. US Secretary of State Alexander Haig exhibited this kind of role confusion in 1981, immediately following an assassination attempt on President Ronald Reagan. Rushing to the White House, Haig announced to the press that "as of now, I am in control here at the White House . . ." (Gilbert, 2000). This in fact was not the case, given the clearly established line of succession, which placed Vice-President George H. W. Bush in charge of the government in the event of the president's disability.

Responsibility is a third organizational role stressor. The two types of responsibility in organizations are for people and for things, such as financial and material resources. Responsibility for people can be especially stressful. Studies reveal that responsibility for people is far more likely to lead to coronary heart disease than is responsibility for things. Being accountable for people usually requires spending more time interacting with others, attending meetings, and attempting to meet deadlines. An early investigation of 1,200 managers linked physical stress to age and level of responsibility (Pincherle, 1972).

Relationships at work

Working and living with other people is one of the most stressful aspects of life. Good relationships between members of a work group are considered a central factor in individual and organizational health. Low trust, low levels of supportiveness, and low interest in problem-solving within the organization characterize poor relationships at work. Further, mistrust is positively related to high role ambiguity, which in turn leads to inadequate interpersonal communications and psychological strain (Sutherland, Cooper, 1999).

Executives with abrasive personalities who threaten colleagues may unwittingly cause stress for others, because they ignore feelings and sensibilities in social interaction (Levinson, 1978). Abrasive personalities are usually achievement-oriented, hard-driving, and intelligent, but they function less well emotionally. Their need for perfection, their preoccupation with themselves, and their condescending, critical style induce feelings of inadequacy among others. Abrasive personalities are both difficult and stressful to deal with; they cause real damage to interpersonal relationships and high stress for subordinates when they are in high positions of responsibility.

Competition among managers and executives is inevitable in organizations; indeed, a certain degree of competition is healthy. Competition, however, can also cause distress, especially if it inhibits one's natural style of behavior. The following case illustrates how colleague competition and a corresponding coping strategy of avoidance were counterproductive. Karen was a middle manager in a medium-sized company:

Karen really wanted to do well at work, but she realized that her male colleagues were threatened by her intellect. They were often sarcastic about her degree in business administration – "Call yourself an administrator; you can't even make coffee without spilling it in the saucer" – it was one joke after another. They liked it best when she was joking and laughing with them and playing the dumb blonde, and she was very good at that. So long as she played the part, she remained popular. But if she attracted the attention of her boss with the speed and quality of her work, then the mockery would start in earnest. So Karen chose to avoid being a success, but she became deeply resentful about playing a role that was not hers. By avoiding success she kept the peace, but in "keeping the peace" she lost her own peace of mind.

This case illustrates how an avoidance strategy for dealing with competitive colleagues can be personally damaging and increase anxiety. What is more productive is to recognize signs that a colleague feels threatened and then identify potential sources of this threat. Signs that a colleague feels threatened include:

● covering up papers on his or her desk when you enter the room

● constantly opposing you at meetings when the boss is present

● hiding important files or materials from you

● undermining you with other colleagues or with the boss

● using memos as a means of conveying lack of trust in you

● noticeably excluding you from office and social functions

● silencing an animated conversation when you enter the room.

Once you have identified that a colleague seems threatened or behaves in an excessively competitive manner, try to identify the reason. Is he or she threatened by your perceived competence, your interest in a particular senior job (which he or she also covets), the boss's relationship with you, or some personality- or management-style incompatibility? Only by identifying the source of the problem can you begin to decide on an appropriate strategy to deal with it. Every strategy chosen has its pluses and minuses; pursue the one with the most pluses.

Career stress and the changing nature of work

Career stress has changed with the changing nature of work, with movement from the old economy to the new economy, and with the process of globalization. Lee Turburn's experience reflects the career stress of the new economy. Lee was a highly successful entrepreneur in the technology sector of the new economy as the founder of Flashnet, an Internet service provider. Lee conceptualized his new business in the mid-1990s, bene-fited from the massive venture capital available in the marketplace, rode the technology sector's rise through an initial public offering of his company, and then watched the sector collapse in the bust of 2000. Lee experienced compressed career stress through Flashnet, which he left before the bust to begin working on a new business idea, which he is now pursuing with ALT Capital Management.

A recent article in *The Economist* featured the potential backlash in the United States against the shift in employment practices resulting from glob-alization. Globalization is leading to higher mobility between employers, to more intrinsic job insecurity, to a short-term-contract culture of employ-ment, and ultimately to the virtual organization. The issue for European businesses is whether they should be traveling in this same direction or, in the words of the Robert Frost poem: "Two roads diverged in a wood, and I – I took the one less traveled by." Europe should take a different and more culturally appropriate path. Europe, and Britain in particular, has moved very far along the path of the Americanization of work, as more and more companies are outsourcing, delayering, utilizing "interim management" and the like, with many more employees, in effect, selling their services to organizations on a freelance or short-term contract basis. This has led to what employers now refer to euphemistically as "the flexible workforce" although in family-friendly terms it is anything but flexible. The psycholog-ical contract between employer and employee in terms of "reasonably per-manent employment for work well done" is truly being undermined, as more and more employees no longer regard their employment as secure and many more are engaged in short-term contracts or part-time work. In one study that encompassed 8 million workers across 400 companies in 17 countries, employment security declined from the mid/late 1980s to the mid/late 1990s. For example, the decline in the United Kingdom was from 70 percent to 48 percent; in Germany 83 percent to 55 percent; in France 64 percent to 50 percent; in the Netherlands 73 percent to 61 percent; in Belgium 60 percent to 54 percent; and in Italy 62 percent to 57 percent. In addition, from the early 1980s to the end of the 1990s the number of men working part time in the United Kingdom has doubled.

In the Institute of Management's Quality of Working Life survey, a range of issues having to do with the changing nature of work in the economy of the United Kingdom were explored, from the impact of major restructuring of work to a long-working-hours culture in industry.

From 1997 to 2000, two out of three of the cohort of 5,000 managers indicated that their organizations underwent major redundancies, 50 percent underwent the introduction of temporary staff, 36 percent the use of contract workers, 37 percent delayering, 34 percent outsourcing, etc. In other words, there had been a steady movement toward a short-term-contract culture in most of these organizations, with managers increasingly selling their services on a less-than-permanent basis. As a consequence of this culture change, managerial loyalty had decreased by 49 percent, morale declined by 64 percent, motivation fell by 53 percent, and job security massively declined by 60 percent.

Much can depend on the executive's career stage. There are three distinctive career stages and needs; expectations and values vary as a function of career stage. In the early years of a career, when the manager is in the establishment phase, there are strong needs for gaining recognition and safety. In the advancement stage, the individual is less concerned with fitting in than with gaining mastery of the organization. Finally, there is a leveling-off during the maintenance stage, as a plateau is reached. Stress factors vary over the career cycle, with implications for health and well-being. For example, in the early years good relationships with the boss are a major concern, but in the advancement phase, co-worker relationships may deteriorate if they are perceived as a threat to prospects for promotion. A preoccupation with the job during advancement might also have a disruptive effect on family life during important developmental years.

Organizational and executive cultures

Organizational culture can be as essential to the success of the business as financial factors. This is especially true in the case of mergers and acquisitions. Executive, management, and employee participation is an essential characteristic of healthy organizational cultures. One bank we worked with in Texas had significant problems with the implementation of their goal-setting and management-by-objectives program, due to the very directive, non-participative style of the chairman of the bank. This stood in marked contrast to the earlier success of a similar goal-setting program in another corporation. The issue of organizational culture is central to managing the merger and acquisition process. In managing cultural differences, Larry Schein has found that stress-and-anxiety-coping skills, such as professionalism combined with high touch and soft ways, are central to addressing issues of work overload and job risk in mergers and acquisitions.

Edgar Schein has taken a deeper look at the executive culture. The executive culture tends to transcend organizational boundaries rather than being isolated to a specific organization. Schein points out that entrepreneurs (e.g., Lee Turburn of Flashnet), founders of organizations (e.g., Herb Kelleher at Southwest Airlines), and members of owning families (e.g., John D. Rockefeller Jr) are more diverse and less typical of the cultural profile developed for promoted CEOs and executives. The assumptions of the executive culture are presented in Table 4.1. The picture that emerges from these assumptions is one of logic and abstraction. The struggle for many executives is around personal issues, interpersonal relationships, and emotional life. On the one hand, they cannot escape these inevitable aspects of the human condition, and, on the other hand, they are not attuned to their own emotional lives in a way that enables them to become familiar and comfortable with the emotional flow of life. Warren Buffett's personal journey in this dilemma is an interesting case in point (Lowenstein, 1995). Buffett was so attuned to making a great American fortune through investments alone that he did not realize for several years that his wife had wallpapered his home study with money wallpaper. In a similar way he was frequently inattentive to his wife and her emotional life, so she moved to the west coast from Omaha and encouraged Warren to find local companionship for himself.

Schein's depiction of the financially focused, embattled lone hero not only resonates with observation and experience, but highlights the insular nature of the executive culture and its lack of openness to those not perceived in some way as peers of equal stature in their own professional rights. With this said, however, there is real danger in drawing conclusions about specific managers or executives based upon assumptions, stereotypical profiles, or the insular nature of the culture. There are concerned and caring executives who somehow achieve a balance between a focus on the financial bottom line and the human side of the enterprise. Gordon Forward exemplifies an executive who fashioned a career based on a genuine concern for people as well as making world-class steel products, leading him to be named one of the top 12 steel-makers of the twentieth century along with Andrew Carnegie and others.

Table 4.1 Assumptions of the executive culture

Financial focus

- Executives focus on the financial survival and growth of the organization to ensure returns to shareholders and to society.
- Financial survival is equivalent to perpetual war with one's competitors.

Self-image: the embattled lone hero

- The economic environment is perpetually competitive and potentially hostile, so the CEO is isolated and alone, appears omniscient and in total control, and feels indispensable.
- Executives cannot get reliable data from subordinates, so they must trust their own judgment.

Hierarchical and individual focus

- Organization and management are intrinsically hierarchical; the hierarchy is the measure of status and success and the primary means of maintaining control.
- The organization must be a team, but accountability has to be individual.
- The willingness to experiment and take risks extends only to those things that permit the executive to stay in control.

Task and control focus

- Because the organization is very large, it becomes depersonalized and abstract and, therefore, has to be run by rules, routines (systems), and rituals ("machine bureaucracy").
- The inherent value of relationships and community is lost as an executive rises in the hierarchy.
- The attraction of the job is the challenge, the high level of responsibility, and the sense of accomplishment (not the relationships).
- The ideal world is one in which the organization performs like a well-oiled machine, needing only occasional maintenance and repair.
- People are a necessary evil, not an intrinsic value.
- The well-oiled organization does not need people, only activities that are contracted.

Home/work pressures

Burke and Greenglass suggest that there is a need for a greater understanding of the reciprocal relationship between work and home domains. Research evidence indicates that job and life satisfaction are influenced by the demands and conflicts of home and family life (Cooper, Lewis, 1997). While home/work pressures can be stressful for any executive, this can be especially challenging for executives who are relocated, especially to an overseas or remote location.

Relocation has become increasingly a necessity for those who want continuous employment, due to changes in the economy and labor market. Managers in the United Kingdom are expected to change their jobs ten to twelve times in their careers. This may require relocation of the family or the need to work away from the home and family for extended periods of time. Although some individuals thrive and cope with this way of life, for many others the experience is stressful and traumatic. If this happens, it becomes a "lose–lose" situation for all concerned – the individuals, the family, the organization and the local community – because close ties are not established or developed.

A study of the stress and strain of job transfer among middle and senior executives indicates that problems for the relocating individual vary according to life stage (Marshall, Cooper, 1979). For example, young, single employees have the pressures of starting a new job and being alone in a strange town or city. They need to build a completely new life structure, without the support of a partner, family or friends, while trying to maintain former contacts. The young marrieds usually have the least constraints, but the dual-career couple faces additional problems when one partner is forced to relocate. Children also find relocation stressful. Infants experience insecurity when their routines are disrupted; older children must become familiar with new schools and learn to make new friends. The partner left at home does not have the organization and related structure of work to help in the building of a new social network and so might be more lonely and unhappy initially.

> Actual relocation is a stressful event; but the decision not to move or accept a transfer may also be a source of pressure, if the individual feels that job security and career aspirations are threatened by their actions.

Guest and Williams found that satisfaction with overseas relocation among executives was strongly influenced by the spouses's adjustment to the move. Actual relocation is, therefore, a stressful event; but the decision not to move or accept a transfer may also be a source of pressure, if the individual feels that job security and career aspirations are threatened by their actions. This is likely to be a significant source of stress for career married women, who tend to feel their family commitments more intensely.

Managing work demands and travel

Some of the pressures executives experience at work are of their own creation; it is possible to develop skills to prioritize work activities, manage interruptions, and deal with difficult colleagues and bosses to achieve a healthier work/personal life balance. In this section we explore some possible solutions to excessive work demands.

Prioritize and set limits on your work

Having a clear sense of priority is central to the effective management of work demands, travel, and work/home balance. During his successful tenure as chairman and CEO of Otis Engineering, a Halliburton company, Purvis Thrash was always very clear that his work was important, but not the most important part of his life; his family and his faith came before his work. While different executives will have different priorities, knowing clearly what one's personal priorities are is very important.

In order to manage your time better it is important to prioritize your activities. But before you can do this you need to analyze how effectively you are working by keeping a time log for a week or two. Audit your time by dividing each day into 15-minute segments, and then at the end of each hour, note the activities you were involved in for each segment. At the end of each day, summarize the time for each activity category. Such details could be entered into a desk diary or recorded by an administrative assistant (Adair, 1982). At the end of the week, again summarize the data to identify the hours spent and the percentage of total time used under key headings.

- *Wasting time?* This helps you to identify *whether* and *where* you are wasting time as well as areas in which you could be better organized or perhaps delegate. Further, if a serious problem of work overload turns up through this work analysis, the time log can help you make a case for more personnel. Regular group meetings at work to discuss current workload and task priorities, particularly if your workload emanates from several different sources, can be useful in gaining the support of others and sharing the workload.

- *Saying "No."* Work overload may also stem from an inability to say "No" or from poor delegation skills. Our need to please others and the feelings of guilt and selfishness we experience when we assert our wishes are often a product of early childhood and cultural upbringing. Parents and teachers tend to reward the compliant rather than the challenging child. If you haven't learned to say "No" and tend to overload yourself, remember what Woody Allen once said: "I don't want to achieve immortality through my work – I want to achieve it by not dying."

Manage interruptions

Two major forms of interruptions that cause significant daily hassles are the telephone and people who intrude on your workspace and time. Executives can minimize telephone interruptions by doing some of the following:

- Batch phone calls.
- Plan what you are going to say or need to know in advance.
- Place a specific time limit on the length of the call.
- Use e-mail, faxes, and other written communication for complex information.
- Use your voicemail during periods of intense work.
- Have a receptionist or administrative assistant screen calls, acting where possible.

North Western Mutual Life, a US insurance company, introduced a "quiet hour" for their employees; all incoming calls were blocked and dealt with by the switchboard. The scheme was so successful that the company reported a 23 percent rise in productivity in one year.

The intrusion of people into your workspace and time can be another real hassle. Some interruptions are a welcome diversion, while too many interruptions are a waste of time, distracting, and irritating. Not all interactions are interruptions. An executive may engage in more than 100 brief interactions in the course of a day. Still, interruptions can be a problem as managers are encouraged to be more accessible to their staff and to adopt open-door policies. Some good strategies for managing interruptions include:

- Establish quiet hours during which you can work undisturbed.
- Establish and make known visiting hours when you are available for drop-ins.

- Arrange meetings away from your desk or office.

- A pleasant smile often suffices for the customary pre- and post-"small talk."

- Do not invite casual droppers-in to sit down; this will encourage them to stay longer.

- Ask unexpected guests how much time is needed; then take the time or schedule an alternative time.

Dealing with a threatened or difficult colleague

Some colleagues feel threatened by powerful executives, and other colleagues are simply difficult to relate to comfortably. In such cases, a positive response or constructive self-talk may help you transform the relationship into a less difficult one. For example, when a colleague constantly criticizes you during meetings, you might wonder, "What is bothering him?" rather than "Why is he such a pain in the neck?" Valid positive responses and constructive self-talk can turn bad experiences into positive relationship experiences with colleagues by thinking differently about stressful situations and by developing self-control. Defensive or negative responses and coping can only inflame a threatened or difficult colleague.

Executives can make choices all the time. What are some of the approaches you can adopt for dealing with threatened or difficult colleagues?

- *Head banger*: Furious anger at being treated in this way. Talk it over with others.

- *Pragmatist*: Accept that it is an unjust fact of life. Get on with your work.

- *Reformer*: Campaign for better decision-making in the firm, involving consultation at shop-floor levels where there is better understanding of the workforce. Discuss your concerns in confidence with respected peers.

- *Alchemist*: Turn base metal into gold. Decide to turn this bad experience into a good one in any way possible. Equip yourself to cope when things do not go your way or get even worse. Make an informed decision to stay and be positive – or leave.

Dealing with a difficult boss

While the "hows" and "whys" of managing subordinates and colleagues at work are common, the same is not true about managing a relationship with the boss – the central relationship in the workplace. Managing bosses requires an awareness of the different types of bosses, their personality needs, and their management styles, and implementing coping strategies that might be most successful in managing them. Here we explore four difficult types of bosses – the bureaucrat, the autocrat, the wheeler-dealer and the reluctant manager (Makin *et al.*, 1988). If you want to influence your own boss, develop a specific profile and be prepared to take offensive or defensive action. As George Bernard Shaw wrote in *Mrs Warren's Profession*:

People are always blaming their circumstance for what they are. I don't believe in circumstances. The people who get on in this world are the people who get up and look for the circumstances they want, and if they can't find them, make them.

- *The bureaucrat* is generally pleasant and mild-mannered but often excessively slow and cautious in making decisions. According to Dean Acheson, former US Secretary of State, the basic rule of the bureaucrat is that memos are sent not to inform the recipient but to protect the sender. You should read all memos from bureaucrats. The best approach for dealing with this type of boss is to know the rules and regulations at work so that you can present proposals consistent with the system.

- *The autocrat* will have very strong views on what ought to be done in any situation. These are derived from their own personal convictions rather than from the organization's rules. They do not listen very well to others. They issue instructions and don't expect to be questioned. Frequently intolerant, they often display great anger in a cold, withdrawn manner. Compliant behavior and personal respect are often effective. Autocrats are difficult to confront.

- *The wheeler-dealer* spends much of his or her time negotiating with other departments over allocation of resources and such matters as purchasing and sales. They leave their departments very much to run themselves. They are impatient and do not "suffer fools gladly." Staff members are not given much guidance, but staff initiative is usually well supported and non-performers ignored. There is a general feeling of dynamism and also a certain amount of chaos. Be prepared to take the initiative, make your own decisions, get on with the task, but keep the boss informed.

● *The reluctant manager,* being technically competent, will generally let their department run itself and do not encourage staff. If a technical problem arises, they offer help if asked and are usually effective. When something non-routine happens, it is difficult to get a decision. They are likely to be high innovators in their technical activities. The main problem with reluctant managers is getting them to engage in interpersonal interactions. Present a number of alternatives from which the manager can choose, strongly supporting your preferred alternative with evidence.

Chapter 4 in a nutshell

1. Executives' health may suffer from work overload or excessive working hours.

2. Litigation, conflict, ambiguity, responsibility, and abrasive personalities cause stress.

3. The changing nature of work causes career stress for executives and managers.

4. Home/work pressures, especially with relocations and dislocations, are an increasing source of stress for executives at work; balance is the key.

5. Skills for managing the demands of work include the ability to prioritize and manage interruptions, while dealing with difficult colleagues and bosses.

5

Professional crisis and personal tragedy

There are no obstacles, only challenges.

Lord Louis Mountbatten, member of the House of Windsor,
killed by the Irish Republican Army

The only thing to fear is fear itself.

Franklin Delano Roosevelt, president of the United States
from 1933 to 1945, led the nation out of the Great Depression
and toward victory in World War II

At 8.45 am on Tuesday, September 11, 2001, American
Airlines Flight 11 crashed into the north tower of the World Trade Center.
Eighteen minutes later, at 9.03 am, United Airlines Flight 175 crashed
into the south tower of the World Trade Center. The largest tenant in
the World Trade Center was Morgan Stanley Dean Witter, with 3,500
employees spread over 20 floors (floors 43–46, 56, 59–74) in the south
tower. This leading investment firm that descended from legendary fin-
ancier J. P. Morgan Sr lost less than 20 employees in this national tragedy,
and only 50 employees were injured. Following the 1993 bombing of the
World Trade Center, Morgan Stanley had put plans into place for such an
emergency, and that readiness saved lives.

In the largest longitudinal study of adult development, George Vaillant
found that every life included in the Grant Study and related projects had
experienced some crisis or tragedy. This was not, however, the distinguishing feature of the lives he studied. Healthy people rose above the
crisis or tragedy. This chapter addresses the wide variety of crises and

tragedies that pose threats to executives' and managers' health, in either the short term or the long term. Managing crisis and tragedy is often best done through collaborative efforts rather than by a single executive acting alone (Gilbert, 2000). These threats fall into two broad categories. One broad category is professional crisis. This category includes political events, terrorism, industrial restructuring activities, labor strife, and industrial accidents. The second broad category is personal tragedy. This category includes the loss of loved ones, loss of financial and material resources, personal tragedies for others, and personal health problems.

When addressing professional crises and personal tragedies, two important distinctions must be made. One is between a broad normal range and extreme stress, while the other is between normal and healthy. This chapter is about extreme pressure, stress, and circumstances that test the edge of the envelope, or go way outside the box, rather than about the broad normal range of executive stress and pressure. Executive life is challenging and stressful, as expected. Business is challenging and hard work, at the executive, managerial, and occupational levels. There are, however, events and circumstances that fall outside the broad normal range of what would be expected in the course of work life. What happened at the World Trade Center on September 11, 2001 is at the extreme, with significant loss of life and damage to health. By its nature, a crisis or a tragedy falls outside the normal range of events.

People who are subject to extreme events run a high risk of having their normal actions and behaviors very disrupted. From a clinical and diagnostic perspective, it can be difficult at times to distinguish between those who have been subjected to extremely stressful events and those who have genetic or developmental limitations. For our purposes, this chapter focuses on healthy, normal executives and managers who have been subjected to extreme or acutely painful experiences as a result of circumstances or events largely beyond their control. The most common result of these events is mental and physical health, though the events take a toll on an executive's resources and energy. These extreme events leave a permanent mark in one's experience, and even in normal, healthy people cause some concurrent or post-experience symptoms such as chest pains, headaches, forgetfulness, or acting out of emotions and feelings.

The second distinction of importance here is that between normal and healthy. What is normal is not always that which is healthy. For example, those working in a stock exchange may find it normal to yell, scream, and shout throughout the course of a day, yet that is not necessarily healthy for one's voice. For this specific case, speech and language pathologists could help an individual develop the breathing, voice projection, and articulation skills to make performance in this context healthier for the individual. What is normal is simply what the norm or standard for behavior is in a particular context or work setting. Normal should be evaluated against the best available information about and standards for what is healthy.

Like at no other time in one's career, an executive in professional crisis or experiencing personal tragedy needs to have an open dialogue going between his or her head and heart, between the cerebral, cognitive processes of thinking and the limbic, emotional processes of feeling. We do not suggest or recommend that executives be ruled by their emotions in the midst of crisis and tragedy. Quite the contrary, crisis and tragedy demand high-quality decisions with the best available information. Being ruled by good decision-making and high-quality thinking processes can yield the best results, yet the failure to recognize and consider one's emotions can result in significant, long-term health problems. Emotions do play a central role in health, whether it is the health of the cardiovascular system or other physiological systems within the body.

Professional crises

There are at least five categories of professional crisis that can place an executive's or manager's health, and even life, at risk. These include political turmoil, terrorism and military action, industrial restructuring activities, labor strife, and industrial accidents. Threats to the business or organization vary in the degree to which they are also, at a more personal level, threats to individual executives or managers. Executives' and managers' health is interdependent with the health of their organizations. While a manager or executive may stay healthy and productive in an unhealthy work environment, to maintain one's health in these environments requires external relationships, anchors, and resources.

Executives, managers, and their families should consider cross-over and spill-over effects too. While some managers and executives may be able to compartmentalize work, home, and other life spheres, the boundaries between these spheres of living are never completely sealed. This means that the effects and threats in one sphere, either at work or at home, can spill-over into the other. The primary concerns in this chapter are with the spill-over effects of professional crises into one's home and family environment and of personal tragedies into one's work and professional life.

Political turmoil

National and international politics affects business operations, exposing an executive to risk, frustration, and even danger. For example, Jack Welch and GE saw their plans to acquire Honeywell frustrated during 2001 because of questions and reservations expressed by European regulators, not because of any questions raised within the US government. The relationship between governmental bodies and business organizations is markedly different in the European Community and in the United States. These differences are not as extreme as in the case between developing and underdeveloped countries where executives and managers work. The health and well-being of executives is at greater risk in the latter.

The political turmoil and change of governments in Iran at the end of the 1970s created special risks and threats for two American executives. In 1975, Electronic Data Systems (EDS) learned that the Ministry of Health in Tehran was looking for a data-processing company experienced in health insurance and social security work. The company made a successful proposal to the ministry and had agreed a contract in August 1976 (Follett, 1983). Paul Chiapparone then became the country manager for the company, as president of EDS Corporation Iran. The internal political context in which Mr Chiapparone and other EDS employees worked began to change dramatically during 1978. The Ayatollah Komeini was committed to the destruction of the Shah of Iran and his Pahlavi dynasty. By late 1978, the political situation in Iran had deteriorated significantly, and the Shah did not have firm control of the country. The political turmoil in the country culminated in the seizing of the US Embassy in Tehran on November 4, 1979, and the taking of 52 Americans as hostages for over a year. The entire episode in Tehran deeply scarred the end of

Jimmy Carter's term as president of the United States, when the rescue effort he mounted came to an ignominious end in the deserts of central Iran.

It was in this context that Mr Chiapparone and his deputy, Bill Gaylord, began what became a harrowing and potentially life-threatening experience at the hands of militant Iranians. The two American executives had their US passports taken, were arrested, and were imprisoned by the Iranian government in December 1978. The US Embassy was of little help in securing their release, due in part to the political turmoil within Iran. President Carter made the decision to send one of his senior US Air Force generals on a secret mission to Tehran (Huyser, 1984). General Huyser entered Tehran in early January 1979 during the last days of the Shah of Iran, saw the transition of power to the Bakhtiar government and the Regency Council, and departed after the return of the Ayatollah Khomeini in early February 1979.

EDS chairman Ross Perot took it upon himself to secure the release of his imprisoned executives, choosing retired Colonel Bull Simons to lead the effort. In contrast to the subsequent, failed rescue attempt of the hostages in the US Embassy in Tehran, Colonel Simons was able to secure the release of the two EDS executives and see them walk safely across the north-west border of Iran into Turkey. A number of senior Iranian military officers followed suit, given the risks to their own lives, evidenced by the fact that other senior Iranian military leaders from the Shah's Government were tried and executed in secret proceedings beginning at midnight and ending before a firing squad at sunrise. Given this history, it is no wonder that when EDS spun off from GM in 1996, the company was still spending $250,000 annually on personal security systems for Mr Chiapparone, who was by then an executive vice-president of EDS.

The political turmoil in Vietnam posed very different pressures and threats for senior American government executives, such as Secretary of Defense Robert McNamara. The threats to McNamara were not personal and immediate in the same way as they were for Chiapparone and Gaylord, and McNamara's personality influenced the health effects of his situation. Robert McNamara was always characterized as a cold and calculated intellect without emotion. He communicated an emotional distance that may have made him a carrier for stress, tension, and health problems, although he did not experience immediate personal health problems. His case is an excellent example of cross-over effects at work. Cross-over effects occur when a person under stress experiences no signs of distress or strain while the spouse sympathetically does. In McNamara's case, his wife's health failed when she got the stomach ulcer that was rightfully his . . .

The pressures of the political turmoil and military failure of the Vietnam War scarred the United States and many who were involved in the war. McNamara almost appeared inhuman in the way he approached the war effort, speaking always in clipped business-like tones and discussing body counts in logical and impersonal ways. While this clearly was a crisis situation for many Americans, American military members, and for the nation, one never quite got that sense from McNamara, who always communicated a sense of control. While he may have bypassed many of the emotions at the time, passing the emotional burden to his wife, he did engage in a soul-searching re-examination of the Vietnam era over 20 years later (McNamara, Vandemark, 1996). Emotions do not necessarily abate with time, and the risks involved in unexamined and unresolved emotion can always reverberate years and decades later in the life cycle. Thus, there is great value in personally confronting and addressing feelings and emotions as they arise.

Terrorism

The crisis that hit the World Trade Center on September 11, 2001 was a surprise to many, yet there had been an early warning call eight years earlier when one of the towers was bombed. Morgan Stanley used the 1993 scare as a learning opportunity to prepare for the future. That decision, coupled with the subsequent planning done within the company, as well as the time-lag between when the aircraft hit the tower and its collapse, may well have saved the lives of thousands of executives, managers, and employees. The majority of civilian executives, managers, and employees do not have the expectation that they are targets for militant armed forces. However, it is precisely the commercial and financial centers that terrorists target, given the fear it engenders and the economic damage it causes. The Dow Jones Industrial Average had its worst one-week decline, over 1,300 points and nearly 14 percent, during the week following the bombing in New York City.

Executives and managers working in less-developed parts of the world are more accustomed to the threats posed by terrorism, thus developing strategies for protection and defense. For example, senior executives living in Nairobi, Kenya, never travel in a single vehicle to the airport at night; instead they always travel with two or more cars at a time. Armed guards and locked family quarters are among the precautionary measures that enhance safety and security, along with 24-hour guards at the perimeter of one's property. Threat assessment, threat monitoring, and planned responses offer some element of preventive action for terrorism.

The aims of terrorists are to intimidate, to create fear, to cause damage, and potentially to extract a price through ransom. The latter occurred in the case of John Paul Getty and his family when one of his grandsons was kidnapped and held for ransom. The threats and the severing of the grandson's ear ultimately came to naught when Getty refused to negotiate, reasoning that this would place other of his grandchildren at risk. Fortunately, the grandson was returned alive, and no subsequent attempts were made to terrorize Mr Getty or his family.

One of the ways in which terrorists strike fear in an organization or a government is to target the senior leadership. Such was the case for the militant Irish extremists who killed Lord Mountbatten, a distinguished member of the House of Windsor, great-grandson of Queen Victoria, and a highly decorated English naval officer. Admiral Earl Mountbatten of Burma served in both World War I and II and was First Sea Lord from 1955 to 1959, when he became chief of the UK defense staff and chairman of the chiefs-of-staff committee. While sailing near his holiday home in County Sligo, Ireland, on August 27, 1979, Mountbatten was murdered by an IRA bomb, which also killed two young boys. Lord Mountbatten's death was a serious psychological blow to the British royal family, yet it did not deter the British government in its policy with regard to the Irish (Ziegler, 1987, 1988, 2001).

Industrial restructuring activities

Industrial restructuring activities, and in particular employment downsizing, have taken a toll on executives and managers in select industries. These activities began during the mid-1980s in the United States and have continued unabated through the present. Employment downsizing occurs when an organization reduces its workforce by more than 5 percent. The majority of American businesses are not currently downsizing, but some industries and sectors of the economy are more vulnerable than are others. Employment downsizing or redundancy is increasingly common in the United Kingdom since Margaret Thatcher began to Americanize the British economy at the beginning of the present period of globalization. Healthcare and banking are two sectors of the US economy that have seen dramatic restructuring activities, in many cases with unpredictable impacts on individual executives.

The savings and loan crisis in the United States and the great Texas banking crash of the 1980s had far-reaching effects on organizations, executives, and managers, many of whom lost their jobs, and in some cases everything which they owned. During the period of 1985 through 1990, Texas lost all but one of its top ten banking institutions, with Banc One, NCNB, Chase, and other national banks and financial institutions from outside the state taking control of their assets with support from the Federal Deposit Insurance Corporation (FDIC). Dr Joseph M. Grant, chairman and CEO of Texas American Bancshares, Inc. (TAB), was one key executive at risk during this period (Grant, 1996). One of the leading banks in Texas, TAB fell during the crash, and Dr Grant was required to turn over the bank's 113-year-old charter to federal banking regulators. While at risk, he did not walk away from the responsibilities he had to his executives and managers, staying through to the very end. He attributed the maintenance of his health to several factors, including his exercise regimen, his sound marriage and family, his close-knit network of peers who backed him, and his sound career plan for the longer term. We would add to that his character and integrity, two cornerstones that enabled him to build very successful post-TAB careers at EDS and Texas Capital Bancshares with support from professional colleagues.

Labor strife

The relationship between management and labor has a complex, at times conflicted, history in which executives, managers, and workers alike may be at risk. During the contentious era of labor-management strife in the US steel industry during the 1920s and 1930s, executives and managers at US Steel were issued 32-caliber pistols for the purpose of self-defense. Both labor and management have at times carried weapons into places of work, placing many at risk of workplace violence. Fortunately, armed conflict is the exception rather than the norm in the history of labor–management relationships.

> During the contentious era of labor-management strife in the US steel industry during the 1920s and 1930s, executives and managers at US Steel were issued 32-caliber pistols for the purpose of self-defense.

A major professional crisis for John D. Rockefeller Jr was the Ludlow massacre, which occurred in October 1913 at the Rockefeller-controlled Colorado Fuel and Iron (CFI) (Chernow, 1998). The Rockefellers' ill-fated involvement with CFI dated back to 1902 when John D. Sr took a 40 percent interest in the company with windfall profits from selling iron ore to US Steel. John D. Sr was militantly anti-union and a major confrontation between CFI's management and its coal workers emerged in 1913 as a result of worker complaints concerning mine safety, pay, and housing conditions. Over 400 miners died in mining accidents during the year. When CFI management failed to respond to worker concerns, 11,000 of the nearly 14,000 miners were on strike by the end of September. Miners and management's guards were heavily armed. The governor sent in Colorado National Guard troops to control the situation. Unfortunately, one shot led to workers being machine-gunned and their tents burned, with over a dozen women and children being killed.

President Wilson intervened with federal troops, who did not leave Colorado until the end of 1914, and John D. Jr was required to testify before the US Congress. There were unsuccessful attempts on his life during this period, but the experience was a touchstone that transformed his attitude toward and relationship with labor. Up until the 1913 labor crisis, John D. Jr had spent much of his life working diligently to rehabilitate the very tarnished family name through the generous philanthropic work of the Rockefeller Foundation. The crisis led him to create a new Department of Industrial Relations at the foundation, transforming both his attitude and behavior in labor–management relationships. For example, when US Steel was unrelenting in its harsh stand on working hours with labor in 1920, John D. Jr sold all his US Steel stock.

Contemporary workplace violence is not divided as much along labor-management lines, and the FBI estimates that 85–90 percent or more of workplace violence is preventable, often being triggered by a stressful event. Labor and management continue to have different objectives and a competitive relationship, yet they must have the capacity for cooperation and collaboration to avoid the kind of crisis experienced by the Rockefellers in 1913. That cooperation is based on open communication and negotiation, on interdependent relationships, and on mutual support. These were illustrated in the both the way John D. Jr worked through the CFI crisis and the way in which Lee Iacocca invited UAW union leader Douglas Frazier on to the Chrysler Corporation Board of

Directors. Building relationships and negotiating conflicts reduces tensions, stress, and risk for all concerned.

Industrial accidents

Industrial accidents are a fifth category of professional crisis that place executives, managers, and employees at risk. Industrial accidents have the clear potential to be life threatening. Many industrial and manufacturing operations require safe operating procedures along with protective clothing, eyewear, and other safety equipment. Danger from heavy equipment and moving parts, while risky for well-trained operators highly familiar with the work environment, may be especially risky for executives or managers unaccustomed to these working conditions. Managers who fail to ensure strict compliance with safety regulations and procedures may ultimately place their own health at risk. Such was the case for a manager in a railcar overhaul facility that failed to discharge an employee after his second safety violation. The manager intervened with senior executives and, rather than terminate the employee, protected his job. Subsequently, the employee committed another safety violation; in this case failing to hook the two sides of a railcar together with a safety chain during overhaul operations. When the manager was in the work area to inspect the operation, one half of the railcar weighing several tons came loose and crushed him to death. Sadly, he had unwittingly contributed to his own death.

The immediate and physical threats from workplace accidents are not the only ones for executives and managers, especially senior executives. Possibly the most lethal industrial accident on record occurred at Union Carbide's Bhopal operations in India on December 3, 1984, where the death toll was approximately 25,000 people (Shrivastava, 1987). Earlier in the century, the explosion of a ship with a cargo of ammonium nitrate in Texas City had been the most lethal, resulting in over 500 deaths. While the government of India labeled the Bhopal crisis an "industrial accident," it was characterized by Union Carbide as an "incident," by the injured victims as a "disaster," and by social activists as a "tragedy" or a "massacre." These very divergent perspectives on the industrial circumstances and events in Bhopal led to equally divergent responses with their associated conflicts, potentially exacerbating an already difficult situation.

The plant managers of Union Carbide (India) Ltd were arrested on criminal charges, as were other Union Carbide officials, including chairman Warren M. Anderson, when they rushed to Bhopal on December 7.

Rather than view Anderson's trip to Bhopal as motivated by concern and sympathy, with clear personal risk to himself, Indian officials and residents perceived his trip as a preemptive effort to minimize Union Carbide's legal responsibility. Anderson did accept moral responsibility for the accident and made significant efforts to enhance communication throughout the crisis.

A less violent form of professional crisis results from economic turmoil and the collapse of a business. The economic turmoil and collapse of Enron, beginning in the fall of 2001, is a sad example of a corporation which had stood in seventh position in the *Fortune 500* list at one point and then experienced a dramatic decline. The decline, beginning with the announcement of a $1 billion write-off and continuing through subsequent revelations of accounting irregularities, led the corporation into bankruptcy court. One of the early casualties in this crisis was J. Clifford Baxter, a senior executive of the corporation who resigned in early 2001 over questions about business irregularities, only to commit suicide, as ruled by the medical examiner, within a year of his departure.

Personal tragedies

Loss of family, friends, financial resources, and health problems are among the personal tragedies that may befall an executive or manager. All executives and managers are vulnerable to such losses and problems, regardless of how well prepared they are. The John Wayne myth suggests that strong men are not vulnerable. The myth is false and a fantasy. The myth was embodied in Harold Geneen's comment when he was chairman of ITT: "If I had enough arms and legs and time, I would do it all myself." Many believe the myth, however, and employees often look to their managers, executives, and leaders to be strong, sure, and secure. The dependency needs of followers lead many executives and managers into the trap of secrecy and lack of disclosure when it comes to personal matters. Franklin D. Roosevelt was a past master at disguising his polio disability, projecting a powerful image of a strong, healthy chief executive.

Loss of loved ones

The loss of loved ones is a personal tragedy that may throw an executive's life out of balance at several levels. Such a life-changing event happened to Hewlett-Packard chairman Lew Platt with the death of his first wife Susan in 1981. In retrospect, the personal tragedy became a growth opportunity for Mr Platt with positive ramifications for Hewlett-Packard as an organization and important effects on HP policies within a decade (Kent, 1998). At the time of Susan's death, Mr Platt was a general manager for the company. For several months following her death, he struggled with the demands of work coupled with caring for his two daughters, aged nine and eleven. He began to realize that many of the struggles of women managers at HP were not of their own making. Prior to her death, Susan Platt had taken the leadership role in all home and family responsibilities. Lew Platt struggled.

Within two years of Susan's death, Lew Platt met and married his second wife Joan, who restored balance to his work and personal life. However, his period of struggle had changed Mr Platt, who continued to empathize with the plight of the women managers and employees at HP who had family and child responsibilities in addition to demanding jobs. As a result, in 1992, when Mr Platt was HP's chief executive and discovered a near mass exodus of women managers from the company, many never to return, and few women rose to senior executive ranks. He also discovered that HP's policies were not flexible enough to accommodate executives' lives outside the workplace. By instituting family-friendly policies, HP became a much more egalitarian work environment for people like Brenda Vathauer, a female marketing manager who returned to work after her maternity leave because HP gave her freedom to set her own agenda.

The positive outcomes from Lew Platt's personal tragedy took time. This was also the case for Lee Iacocca when his wife Mary died. He too was thrown out of balance and struggled in his personal life, marrying twice and briefly over the several years following her loss, before finding a new equilibrium in life.

Loss of financial and material resources

The great Texas banking crash of the 1980s was a time through which executives lost significant financial and material resources. The state of Texas lost hundreds of thousands of jobs, and all the major Texas banks lost their independence, with the exception of Frost Bank (Grant, 1996). Joseph M. Grant was one of those executives who experienced significant financial and material loss as chairman and CEO of Texas American Bancshares, Inc. At the trough of the tragedy, Dr Grant had to turn over TAB's 113-year-old bank charter to officials of the FDIC (Federal Deposit Insurance Corporation). There were a number of preventive health management strategies that Dr Grant pursued during this very difficult time in his life. Two of the central anchors that secured his health were the top team of executives who stood with him through the final days at TAB and the personal/professional friendships that backed him financially until he was able to get his banking career back on a positive track. He was able to do this through his years as chief financial officer for EDS and now as chairman and CEO of Texas Capital Bancshares in Dallas, Texas.

Personal tragedies for others

In her autobiography, Katharine Graham, the late chairman of *The Washington Post*, describes the pain in the workplace caused by the manic-depressive episodes of her late husband Philip during his tenure as president and publisher of the *Post* (Graham, 1997). He ultimately shot himself to death in 1963, leaving his wife Katharine ill-equipped to assume responsibility for the paper her father had established and then brought Philip Graham in to run. As Lew Platt did, Katharine Graham turned a personal tragedy into a positive growth experience, if a difficult one. Through years of challenge and growth, she left a life legacy of personal strength and professional integrity. She is not alone as an executive who came to grips with personal tragedy, rose above it, grew stronger, and ultimately realized the potential within herself only previously imagined.

Health problems

Vulnerabilities can become problems in difficult economic times. This was the case for Theodore John "Ted" Arneson, who founded Professional Instruments Corporation, an engineering firm, in 1946 (Tanonye, 2001). Mr Arneson experienced a serious depression in 1969 as a result of a financial crisis in which interest rates rose, banks called in loans with lower rates, and big clients canceled contracts. These business reverses overwhelmed him, though he was able to see himself and the business through safely. However, this was just an early-warning indicator, and when times got tough seven years later, Mr Arneson attempted to commit suicide. Fortunately, his failed attempt led to psychological intervention as well as support from family and friends. Although he was still chairman of the board in 2001, his three sons were running the business, and much of his personal time was devoted to suicide prevention.

Mike Welch's experience during his tenure as chairman and CEO of Tenneco was not as fortunate. Mr Welch developed brain cancer and continued his leadership role in the company during a period of very rigorous, challenging treatments. His battle with cancer was one he finally lost, which is still too often the case.

The silver lining?

Professional crises and personal tragedies are the dark clouds that drift over executives' lives. Every cloud does not have a silver lining, and it would be unrealistic to think so. These are experiences with which few of us are comfortable, yet they are experiences that all executives must be prepared to cope with and to manage. While the last thing a good soldier wants to do is go to war, it is the first thing that he or she is prepared to do. By the same token, the last thing an executive wants to manage is a professional crisis or personal tragedy, yet in the framework of preventive health management, it is one of the first experiences he or she should be prepared to confront. As we have seen, it is sometimes in the midst of professional crisis or personal tragedy that we discover more of who we are and what our real strengths are, so as to grow more fully into adulthood. In the words of Rudyard Kipling:

> The last thing a good soldier wants to do is go to war, it is the first thing that he or she is prepared to do. By the same token, the last thing an executive wants to manage is a professional crisis or personal tragedy, yet in the framework of preventive health management, it is one of the first experiences he or she should be prepared to confront.

[...]
If you can meet with triumph and disaster,
And treat these two imposters just the same; [...]
Or watch the things you gave your life to broken,
And stop and build 'em up with wornout tools; [...]
Yours is the Earth and everything that's in it,
And – which is more – you'll be a man, my son!

Taken from his poem 'If', (1910) *Rewards and Fairies*

Chapter 5 in a nutshell

1. Executives and managers should expect to experience some professional crisis or personal tragedy at some point throughout their career.

2. The crisis or tragedy may well be an opportunity for growth and can be overcome.

3. Never take it personally; you are not the first one to experience crisis or tragedy.

4. Always ask for the help you need from the most experienced experts available.

5. Plan ahead for your career and your organization, and then live one day at a time.

Part III

Building strength and balance

6

Physical health

I wish to preach, not the doctrine of ignoble ease,
but the doctrine of the strenuous life.

Theodore Roosevelt, US President, speaking in 1899

Our growing softness, our increasing lack of physical fitness,
is a menace to our security.

John F. Kennedy, US President, 1960

People who say they can't find the time to become fit should
realize that a fitness program actually produces time.

Dr George Sheehan

People who don't know how to keep themselves healthy
ought to have the decency to get themselves buried, and not
waste time about it.

Henrik Ibsen, Norwegian dramatist, late nineteenth century

Physical health is a cornerstone for executive strength, energy
and performance. The pressures and stresses of the executive lifestyle can,
however, have an adverse impact on an executive's physical health, as we
saw in Chapter 2. Heart attacks are the most serious physical threats to
health executives face. Dwight D. Eisenhower's heart attack, Jerry Junkins's
sudden death, and Jack Welch's angioplasty all illustrate the point. To safeguard this cornerstone of their health, executives need to guard against cardiovascular risks with heart-healthy behavior, enhance their physical fitness,

and follow a proper diet. These three keys to physical health can be supplemented with additional strategies for healthy living.

United States President Theodore Roosevelt found bodily vigor and physical health to be the foundation upon which the intellect and character stood. Physical stamina and love of outdoor sports were the hallmark of his remarkable character. His promotion of the "strenuous life" was his lifelong preoccupation. "Teddy" Roosevelt's robust physical energy and prowess did not come naturally; they were the result of great effort, disciplined choice and striving. Roosevelt grew up a sickly child, suffering from asthma and bad eyesight. He did not, however, accept those characteristics as a life's trajectory. Rather, as a young man, Roosevelt devoted himself to vigorous exercise and weight-lifting, gaining physical strength, stamina, and vitality. His second wife Edith had a tennis court built for him at the White House, and he continued to pursue vigorous exercise and outdoor activities throughout his lifetime (Morris, 2001).

Heart-healthy lifestyle

Coronary heart disease is the single biggest threat to executive health and well-being. The lives of Dwight D. Eisenhower, Jerry Junkins, Jack Welch, and countless other executives and leaders, as well as the epidemiological data presented in Chapter 2, provide stark testimonies to this reality. At the same time, a "heart-healthy lifestyle" can add literally years of active, productive life. This means taking a proactive approach to develop a healthy lifestyle, to identify and manage medical risk factors, and to address issues of personality and stress. Most actions to reduce the chance of heart attack also reduce the chance of stroke and other cardiovascular complications.

Managing cardiovascular risk factors

Reducing the risk of heart attacks and strokes requires three basic actions:

- undergo routine medical checkups to identify and manage risk factors
- maintain a heart-healthy lifestyle
- confront stress and personal traits that put you at risk.

Direct and indirect risk factors for the development of coronary heart disease and related cardiovascular conditions include high blood pressure, blood lipid disorders, diabetes, smoking, overweight and obesity, physical inactivity, lack of social support, hostile personality, and perhaps the Type-A behavior pattern, as noted in Chapter 2. Several of these risks, including high blood pressure and blood lipid disorders have a genetic component. Though these genes cannot (yet) be modified, their adverse affects can often be greatly reduced by actively managing their clinical effects.

Routine medical checkups and management of identified risk factors is the first line of defense. The American Heart Association, the American Academy of Family Practice, the European Society of Cardiology, the World Health Organization, and other bodies, have developed recommendations for routine screening for cardiovascular risk factors. High blood pressure, blood lipid disorders, and diabetes are all risk factors which initially and in their milder forms often can be successfully treated with regular physical exercise and changes in diet. For each of these conditions there also now exist safe, effective medications which have been shown to prevent heart attacks and save lives. Hence, regular medical checkups and adherence to prescribed treatment are essential for executive health.

A heart-healthy lifestyle can add years to your life as well as life to your years. According to the task force of the European Society of Cardiology on "Prevention of Coronary Heart Disease in Clinical Practice" (Wood *et al.*, 1998) and a recent review of the literature on prevention of coronary heart disease by diet and lifestyle (Kromhout *et al.*, 2002) there are four key lifestyle recommendations which, if followed, could substantially reduce cardiac deaths:

● Don't smoke.

● If you use alcohol, do so in moderation.

● Be moderately to vigorously physically active at least 30 minutes each day.

● Maintain a healthy diet and weight control.

Each of these lifestyle recommendations has important benefits for overall health in addition to the specific benefits for reducing heart attacks. Each is explored separately later in this chapter.

Job stress

Stress – particularly work stress – is implicated as a risk factor in coronary artery disease (British Heart Foundation, 2002). Russek and Zohman compared young coronary patients between 25 and 40 years of age (some with confirmed myocardial infarctions, others with only angina pectoris) with healthy controls and found that 91 percent of the coronary patients reported prolonged stress related to work responsibility, compared to only 20 percent of the controls. They found that 25 percent were previously coping with two jobs, an additional 46 percent had been working 60 hours or more per week, and 20 percent reported frustration, discontent, insecurity or inadequacies associated with their jobs. Wolf found similar reports of dissatisfaction and dejection among myocardial infarction patients compared to a matched control group. A marked variability in blood pressures (both systolic and diastolic) was observed in those with coronary heart disease, and this was most marked among those who subsequently died from coronary heart disease. This psychophysiological responsiveness to emotional stress is referred to as reactivity. The research results seem to show that temperament and behavior are risk factors for coronary disease (Byrne, 1987).

A 1999 review in the *British Medical Journal* of prospective studies of psychosocial factors in the etiology and prognosis of coronary heart disease found a significant relationship between work-related stress and coronary heart disease (Hemingway, Marmot, 1999). Chapter 7 addresses specifically a preventive approach to work stress.

Mike Goldsmith

Mike Goldsmith, a UK businessman, described in a national newspaper (*Independent*, 1991) the terrible shock of experiencing a heart attack:

There is almost always a warning, but hospital beds and graveyards are full of people who couldn't or wouldn't recognize it. I'd had scares – what hypochondriac hasn't? – but none was like the real thing.

Mike Goldsmith had no idea what was happening to him and was extremely unwilling to admit how it had happened:

Back home, after a short stay on a general ward, I tried to come to terms with what had happened to me. We have no family history of heart disease; my diet, deliberately, didn't contain much fat, and my evenings almost always included a workout on my weight bench. The answer had to be stress. At a stress management course I'd attended a few weeks before I'd been the only one to say I had no problems. That was my problem.

I worked in local government and there had been some restructuring that had been a big disappointment for me. After the shake-up I'd had to cover two other jobs that had not been filled immediately and train new staff . . . At home I had started to build a large extension to our house, involving endless negotiations with planning and building officials. Then there were the French lessons, and the driving lessons I was giving my son. During the year my wife's parents had died. I had been attached to both of them.

But I had remained calm and unruffled. Everyone else might lose their cool but I was always in control. In the end my body told me where to stuff my self-control.

Mike Goldsmith was lucky. He survived. Moreover, his impressive honesty and willingness to change his lifestyle are a striking example to follow.

Coronary-prone behavior and hostility

Chief executives and others in highly demanding, achievement-oriented positions must also consider the effects of stress and personality on heart health. As early as 1910, Sir William Osler noted that angina pectoris was especially common among successful members of the business community, and he attributed this, in part, to their hectic pace of life. Even a century earlier, Jean Nichols Corvisart des Marets (1755–1821), an eminent cardiologist who was said to have founded cardiac symptomatology and described the mechanics of heart failure (1806), observed that heart disease had two principle causes, from the action of the organ and from the passions of man. The passions Corvisart des Marets noted included anger, madness, fear, jealousy, despair, joy, avarice, cupidity, ambition, and revenge.

In their pioneering work in the 1970s, Meyer Friedman and Ray Rosenman found that coronary patients were extremely competitive, high-achieving, aggressive, hasty, impatient and restless. They were characterized by explosive speech patterns, tenseness of facial muscles, and appearing to be under pressure of time and the challenge of responsibility. The two cardiologists labeled this the "Type-A behavior pattern" (TABP) in contrast to the low coronary-heart-disease risk behavior which they labeled Type B. Type-A behavior has been found to be more prevalent in high-status jobs. One study looked at 943 white-collar, middle-class males in Buffalo, New York. The men came from five different work settings: the administrative and professional staff of a state health agency, supervisory personnel from a public service organization, officers from industrial and trade unions, faculty at a major private university, and administrative officers of a large banking corporation. Type-A behavior was significantly related to status as measured by rank, level of occupational prestige and income, and also to rapid career achievement in rank and income relative to age (Mettlin, 1976).

Though evidence from the 1970s and early 1980s supported the TABP as a significant independent psychosocial behaviorial risk factor for coronary heart disease, subsequent large-scale and prospective studies have failed to demonstrate clear evidence for TABP as a coronary-heart-disease risk factor. To explain these negative findings, several studies have tried to determine whether there is a "coronary-prone" component of the Type-A pattern. Theodore M. Dembroski first proposed the "potential for hostility" as the most likely "toxic" component of Type A.

Hostility is seen as a personality trait characterized by a "stable attitude of ill will and negative evaluation of people and events." It may include negative beliefs about others, expressions of disgust and contempt, and even overt aggression (Mendes de Lwon, Meesters, 1991). There is now a growing body of evidence indicating that hostility is indeed a more reliable predictor of coronary heart disease than TABP, and today this still holds true. A 1996 analysis (Miller *et al.*) of 45 studies found a significant relationship between structured interview indicators of hostility and coronary heart disease. Among six prospective studies using the Cook–Medley hostility subscore of the Minnesota Multiphasic Personality Index (MMPI), three have found clear associations between hostility and coronary artery disease (Leupker, 1998). These studies have focused

Figure 6.1 Type-A questionnaire

Can wait patiently	1 2 3 4 5 6 7 8 9 10 11	Impatient while waiting
Takes things one at a time	1 2 3 4 5 6 7 8 9 10 11	Tries to do many things at once, thinks about what will do next
Slow deliberate talker	1 2 3 4 5 6 7 8 9 10 11	Emphatic in speech fast and forceful
Cares about satisfying him/ herself no matter what others may think	1 2 3 4 5 6 7 8 9 10 11	Wants good job recognized by others
Slow doing things	1 2 3 4 5 6 7 8 9 10 11	Fast (eating, walking)
Easy-going	1 2 3 4 5 6 7 8 9 10 11	Hard driving (pushing yourself and others)
Expresses feelings	1 2 3 4 5 6 7 8 9 10 11	Hides feelings
Many outside interests	1 2 3 4 5 6 7 8 9 10 11	Few interests outside work/home
Unambitious	1 2 3 4 5 6 7 8 9 10 11	Ambitious
Casual	1 2 3 4 5 6 7 8 9 10 11	Eager to get things done

Plot total score below

Type B   Type A
14   84   154

Scoring

The higher the score achieved in this questionnaire, the more firmly an individual can be classified as Type A. For example, 154 points is the highest score and indicates the maximum Type-A coronary-prone personality. It is important to understand that there are no distinct divisions between Type A and Type B: people fall somewhere on a continuum leaning more toward one type than the other. An average score is 84. Anyone with a score above that is inclined toward Type-A behavior, and below that toward Type-B behavior.

almost exclusively on men; little information is available on the relationship of hostility and coronary artery disease among women. Some studies have indicated that it is the expression of anger-hostility, not its mere experience, that is positively related to the severity of coronary artery disease. The Hostile Attitude Scale (HAS), an easily administered measure of hostility, is presented in Table 6.1. At least one published study has found significant correlation between the HAS and angiographic evidence of coronary artery disease (Arthur *et al.*, 1999).

Enhancing heart-healthy behavior

Though evidence on the overall impact of the TABP is mixed, at least one study found that helping people at high risk to change their behavior pattern resulted in reduced risk of recurrent heart attacks (Friedman *et al.*, 1984). Though the Type-A pattern is often associated with the successful hard-driving executive, there is some evidence that the most successful professional people are more similar to the Type-B personality than Type A. That is, the most successful men were not hard-driving, aggressive and competitive, but rather they were relaxed and possessed a warmth that attracted others. Friedman and Rosenman offer a number of strategies to manage elements of Type-A behavior. These includes strategies against the "hurry sickness", strategies to focus on what attitudes and outlooks it is worth having, and strategies against hostility. The strategies against hostility include the following four daily "drills" (Friedman, Rosenman, 1974):

1. Monitor your own hostile attitudes and behaviors. Remind yourself of your hostility and inclination to flare up. "Try throughout the day to enhance your awareness of the wants and needs of your friends as you simultaneously strive to diminish your own sensitivity to possible affronts."

2. Speak genuine words of thanks and appreciation to others who have performed well.

3. Stop talking about your ideals and your disappointments as though few other people have ideals. "Most so-called 'idealists' are frustrated and hostile little gods . . ." Avoiding finding fault and blaming others for failures or disappointments.

4. Smile at as many people as you can as often as you can. Look for qualities in other people that engender respect, admiration or affection.

> If you exhibit Type-A behavior – especially the hostility component – you did not develop it in a week or two. To change this pattern of behavior may require months or even years to re-engineer.

If you exhibit Type-A behavior – especially the hostility component – you did not develop it in a week or two. To change this pattern of behavior may require months or even years to re-engineer, yet the effort to improve physical health and minimize the risk of a heart attack can be well worth the investment.

Physical fitness

Physical fitness through regular physical activity is the second key to an executive's physical health. The positive effects of regular exercise on health and well-being are so broad that, if one were to bottle physical exercise and sell it on the street, the label would read much like the labels "snake oils" and "cure-all tonics" of the nineteenth century. Yet the scientific evidence is overwhelming for a wide range of benefits for psychological and physical health. These benefits occur for children, the young, and adults of all ages.

Regular physical exercise substantially reduces both the frequency and fatality of heart attacks; delays the onset of high blood pressure and reduces blood pressure in people with hypertension; contributes to weight control; helps to maintain a healthy balance of blood lipids; reduces the risk of colon cancer; lowers the chance of developing adult diabetes and reduces mortality in those who do develop diabetes; promotes psychological well-being; improves mood and relieves symptoms of anxiety and depression; maintains musculoskeletal strength and flexibility; and improves overall functioning and reduces the risk of falling in older people (US Department of Health and Human Services, 1996). Long-term studies show, for example, that the risk of coronary heart disease for physically active people is roughly half that of inactive people (Powell *et al.*, 1987).

In addition to these well-proven effects, there is some evidence that, among other effects, regular physical activity may reduce the risk of developing depresssion; the occurrence of breast, prostate, and other cancers; and the development of osteoporosis in post-menopausal women.

For the executive dealing with high levels of stress, exercise reduces the physiological consequences of stressful situations, alters mood states in the short-term, and personality traits (e.g., anxiety and depression) in the long term (Bortner, 1969). Engaging in regular exercise may decrease the level of physiological arousal which occurs during stressful situations and help to induce a state of relaxation. The exact psychological and physiological processes, however, that exercise contributes to stress management are not fully understood.

Aerobic exercise has received the most praise as a stress antidote. Through aerobic exercise, the individual's heart and respiration rates are sustained at a high level for 20 to 30 minutes. Jogging, brisk walking, aerobic dancing, and swimming are all aerobic exercises. Aerobic exercise is the one form of exercise that can predictably achieve cardio-respiratory fitness. Recreational sports such as squash and tennis can all be excellent ways of releasing tension and frustration, but they do not provide the aerobic benefits. Similarly, many people find that a favorite activity or hobby, such as gardening, sewing, listening to music, or soaking in a hot bath, can be tremendously helpful in releasing the build-up of tension. The key to such activities is that they can be done purely for the pleasure they bring. Although such traditional methods of relaxing have received little attention from researchers, many people know that engaging in an favorite activity can help repair the ravages of the day.

Core elements of physical fitness

There are three dimensions to physical fitness: cardiovascular fitness (also known as aerobic fitness or endurance), muscle flexibility, and muscle strength. Each core element of physical fitness (aerobic fitness, muscle flexibility, and muscle strength training) makes an independent contribution to the physical health of an executive. These aspects of physical fitness may be achieved in various ways. For example, recreational sports and activities such as bowling, softball, horseback riding, racket games, gardening, and chopping wood, may all contribute to physical fitness, and may also serve as physical outlets for stress-induced energy, frustration, and aggression. There are specific benefits in these various forms of physical activity as well as benefit tradeoffs of various alternatives.

● *Aerobic fitness* refers primarily to the cardiovascular fitness achieved through endurance training, such as running and bicycling. Aerobic exercise is any form of repetitive physical activity that produces a sustained heart rate, respirations, and metabolic rate for a period of at least 20 to 30 minutes. Jogging, swimming, aerobic dance, brisk walking, rowing, continuous bicycling, vigorous tennis or other racket games, and cross-country skiing are examples of such exercise. Aerobic exercise/endurance training must involve the large muscle groups and be rhythmic and continuous. This is the one form of exercise that predictably achieves cardiovascular fitness. Among young adults, one eight-week aerobic training program found that enhanced parasympathetic nervous system activity and decreased central nervous system laterality were mechanisms underlying certain aerobic training effects (Kubitz, Landers, 1993).

Physical exercise has emotional, psychological, and physiological benefits. A study of 11 young adult male athletes found that aerobic power and body size influenced exercise-induced stress hormone responses in different environmental conditions. So, consider environmental conditions when designing your exercise program. The effects of physical exercise on one's response to mental stress are mixed; one study rejected the training as beneficial in physiological responsiveness to mental stress (Steptoe *et al.*, 1993). A longitudinal Dutch study of men found that regular exercise did not increase the resistance to stress-related disorders (deGeus *et al.*, 1993). However, in a study of 48 women, aerobic exercise was found to dampen physiological reactivity while reducing anxiety-related thoughts (Rejeski *et al.*, 1992). This is consistent with research showing that jogging and the relaxation response were consistently more effective for women than men (Berger *et al.*, 1988). There are, however, no long-term benefits from single sessions of jogging, which suggests the importance of maintaining the discipline of jogging to receive continuing benefits.

> Physical exercise has emotional, psychological, and physiological benefits. A study of 11 young adult male athletes found that aerobic power and body size influenced exercise-induced stress hormone responses in different environmental conditions.

● *Muscle flexibility* is a second dimension of physical fitness central to developing optimum physical health. Flexibility is attained through milder forms of physical fitness training, which may also be very important to individual preventive stress management. Because of the redirection of blood flow to the brain and large muscle groups in stressful circumstances, there is a need for a counter effect aimed at achieving flexibility and muscular relaxation through regular, rhythmic routines which are not necessarily intense enough to produce cardiovascular conditioning. Simple calisthenics and muscle-toning exercises, modern dance, the recently popular traditional Chinese system of symbolic movements known as Tai Chi Chuan, and other systems of eastern origin such as Hatha yoga and Aikido are all examples of ways to achieve muscle flexibility. Neck and Cooper recommend stretching three times per day in a slow, gradual, and even manner, focusing additional attention on tight muscles that need 50 percent more stretching. If you have experienced an injury, heat up the muscle or tendon before stretching and activity.

Muscle stretching and flexibility training can go hand in glove with relaxation training, because both of these practices lower subjective and objective states of arousal. Tai Chi, a moving meditation, is characterized as a moderate physical exercise activity, which may have superior effects in recovery from stressful events. During a six-week study in an electronics assembly plant, modest improvements in mood and flexibility were found as the result of a daily ten-minute strength and flexibility program (Prank *et al.*, 1995). Muscle flexibility and strength are related in that it is difficult to develop full strength in tense muscles that lack flexibility.

- *Muscle strength training*, a third dimension of physical fitness, may be central to the successful management of certain specific demands or stressors. For example, US Air Force pilots who were put on a weight-training program for increasing muscle strength were able to tolerate higher G-forces, caused by high linear accelerations in fighter aircraft such as the F-15 Strike Eagle, than pilots in an aerobic training program or control group. Hence, some occupations and work tasks require muscle strength for successful performance. By itself, this form of exercise does not usually achieve cardiopulmonary conditioning, but it can be quite effective in venting hostilities, relaxing tense muscles, and building self-image. Further, such strength training increases muscle mass, which can boost the rate at which the body burns calories. At least one study found that muscle strength training (i.e., anaerobic exercise) did not produce as positive a set of outcomes as aerobic training did (Norris *et al.*, 1990).

Jody Grant – fitness through difficult transitions

With an MBA and a PhD in finance and economics, Joseph M. (Jody) Grant has led a distinguished, if challenging career. Among many business and community responsibilities, Grant also served as International President of the Young Presidents' Organization (YPO). The YPO is composed of individuals who became president or CEO of qualifying companies prior to their 40th birthday. An All-American swimmer in college, Grant has continued to swim recreationally, broadened his interest to run, and completed several marathons. He has weathered two major career crises, throughout which he maintained his program of regular exercise. The first was the bankruptcy in the great Texas banking crash of the 1980s of Texas American Bancshares, where Grant had been CEO and president. The second was his transition out of the EDS Corporation, where he had been chief financial officer, when EDS was spun off by GM. Since EDS, Grant has served as chairman and CEO of Texas Capital Bankshares, a successful commercial bank serving a wide range of mid-sized companies. Grant credits his fitness program for helping him to maintain his health, keep a positive outlook, and emerge successfully from two major career adjustments.

Five excuses for avoiding regular exercise

The level of physical activity recommended by the US Department of Health and Human Services (2001) to achieve substantial health benefits is five or more times per week of moderately intense activity such as brisk walking for 30 minutes or more per occasion. The same effect can be achieved with shorter sessions of more strenuous activities (such as 15 to 20 minutes of jogging) as with longer sessions of moderately intense activity. Additional benefits seem to occur with greater amounts of activity.

Tom Monaghan, founder of Domino's Pizza; Judy Kaplan, former CEO of Action Products International; Dr Thomas Frist Jr, chairman and CEO of Columbia/HCA Healthcare; Charles O. Rossotti, commissioner of the US Internal Revenue Service; and Julian C. Day, chief financial officer for Sears, Roebuck & Company all engage in regular physical exercise, ranging from jogging three times a week to daily runs of five miles, to marathons and half-marathons (Neck, Cooper, 2000). These executives speak of the benefits they gain in terms of energy, concentration, decision-making ability, confidence, and overall well-being.

Despite the clear benefits of physical activity which are documented by researchers and reported first hand by fit executives, between one-third and two-thirds of executives and senior managers in the US and Europe are not exercising regularly. Why? Here are five common arguments against exercise, and a brief counter-argument to each:

1. *I don't have time . . . It takes precious time from work, family, or other commitments.* Many if not most people who exercise regularly find that they actually gain time through increased alterness, mental problem-solving during exercise, and other benefits.

2. *I get bored running.* Fitness can come from a variety of individual or group activities, including walking, swimming, bicycling, basketball, volleyball, touch football, vigorous garden work, dancing fast (social), raking leaves. Mixing different forms of exercise on different days and varying routes for walking, running, or biking will help. Some executives use early-morning runs to explore new cities they are visiting.

3. *I've got a bad knee (bad back, etc.).* Some physical problems are severe enough to prevent any vigorous activity. Usually, however, it is a matter of chosing a form of exercise which fits your limitations. Certainly for many forms of chronic back pain and other musculoskeletal problems, exercise actually helps overcome or control pain and stiffness. If in doubt, you should see your healthcare provider.

4. *There's never a convenient time . . . It's always dark out when I leave – either in the morning when I go to work, or the evening when I come home . . . I travel too much.* People who maintain regular exercise have found the best fit within their schedule. It may be a matter of trial and error. It may require changing morning or evening habits or your attitude about running in the dark.

5. *How could I even start? I get winded just going up two flights of stairs.* For previously inactive people, the key is to start slowly with short sessions of five to ten minutes and gradually build up to the desired level over a period of several weeks.

The adverse effects of exercise are few. Musculoskeletal injuries can generally be prevented by progressive conditioning, rather than a sudden increase in the level of physical activity. Falls, injuries from motor vehicles, attacks by dogs, injuries from contact sports, heart attacks and other serious cardiovascular events can occur with strenuous exercise; but the overall effect of regular exercise is to reduce the risk of death from heart disease. To reduce the risk of adverse effects, the American College of

Sports Medicine (ACSM) recommends that inactive people who begin an exercise program should start gradually and work up. In addition, people with serious health problems, those with cardiovascular risks such as high blood pressure, men over age 40, and women over age 50 should see their healthcare provider before starting a program of signficantly increased activity.

Healthy eating and weight control

Poor diet and excess body weight are important risk factors for cardiovascular disease, as noted earlier. In addition, it is likely that one-third of cancers can be prevented by maintaining a healthy diet, normal weight and physical activity throughout one's life, according to the World Health Organization.

Because overweight and obesity result from an imbalance between calorie consumption and calorie intake, the most effective weight management is a combination of exercise and reasonable eating. In the absence of exercise, dieting stimulates a "starvation reflex" whereby the body's metabolic rate is decreased. This means that dieting alone decreases calorie consumption.

A combination of sensible eating and regular exercise has the best record of long-term success for losing excess weight and maintaining the loss. Increasing calorie consumption by 500 calories per day (roughly equivalent to jogging four miles) while at the same time reducing intake by 500 per day (one Big Mac) would typically result in weight loss of two pounds per week.

> While much controversy exists about certain questions on diet and health, most stress researchers appear to agree about the value of eating in such a way as to maintain level energy reserves through the day and to keep weight at a proper level.

While much controversy exists about certain questions on diet and health, most stress researchers appear to agree about the value of eating in such a way as to maintain level energy reserves through the day and to keep weight at a proper level. The age-old adage – moderation in all things – seems to be sound advice today. Large amounts of sugar, processed foods, alcohol, and caffeine have been connected with poor overall health, irregular energy patterns and lowered resistance to illness and stress. Increasing awareness of the possible relationship between certain foods and allergies, delinquent behavior, anxiety, headache, tension, and fatigue are reported.

Rippere describes a wide variety of adult psychiatric problems that have been associated with nutrient deficiencies, food allergies, food addictions, and caffeine intake. As she points out, it is pointless to refer an individual to relaxation training while their caffeine intake, from coffee, tea, chocolate, and cola, is around one gram per day. While people with unusual or persistent symptoms may require professional evaluation, for the majority of us, eating patterns should reflect a well-balanced diet that maintains body weight within medical guidelines. This perhaps is easier said than done, because we are often controlled by the pressures of society and wooed by media images of how we should look. Again it is necessary to emphasize a need for self-awareness, of what we are and what we can reasonably expect to become. Non-compliance to a diet or an exercise regimen is usually the result of trying to adhere to totally unrealistic goals.

What you eat can have an impact on attention span, memory, and mood, similar to the effect of drugs. Studies have shown that a high-carbohydrate, low-protein meal induces a relaxed mood and reduced mental acuity, while a low-carbohydrate, high-protein meal does the opposite (Spring *et al.*, 1982–83). When you eat is also of importance. A stable flow of blood sugar is essential for responding to stressors effectively. The brain needs a steady flow of glucose to function properly. The body utilizes nutrients more efficiently with four or five small meals a day. Individuals who ingest the bulk of their caloric intake in one large evening meal risk weight gain and increased cholesterol levels.

Chronic stress is associated with increased blood-cholesterol levels, a risk factor for heart disease and other maladies. Research by Dean Ornish has shown that managing stress helps lower blood cholesterol levels and reverses obstructions in blood vessels. Along with stress management, Ornish prescribes a very low-fat diet for reversing heart disease. His studies have indicated that a diet in which fat is limited to less than 10 percent of total calories, combined with the use of stress-management activities for one hour per day, can reverse the progression of heart disease. Ornish's reversal diet consists of 10 percent fat, 70 to 75 percent carbohydrate, 15 to 20 percent protein, and 5 milligrams of cholesterol per day. His prevention diet is similar, with fats no more than double the amount in the reversal diet. Ornish recommends that total cholesterol be kept lower than 150, and the ratio of total cholesterol to high-density lipoprotein (HDL) be less than 3.0; HDL is the healthy cholesterol.

Researchers (Kromhouf *et al.*, 2002) from the Netherlands, Italy, Belgium and Spain summarize work of the the European Society of Cardiology, American Heart Association, the National Cholesterol Education Program, and other international analyses in terms of the following critical dietary recommendations for the prevention of heart attacks, strokes, and other cardiovascular problems:

● Keep an energy balance for weight control (indicated by a body mass index below 25 kg/m²).

● Consume <10 percent of energy from saturated fat.

● Eat (fatty) fish at least once a week.

● Eat at least 400 grams of vegetables and fruits per day.

● Limit salt consumption to less than 6 grams per day.

The following ten steps comprise a comprehensive but simple prescription for a healthy diet that enhances the ability to cope with stress (Davis *et al.*, 1995).

1. Eat a variety of foods.

2. Maintain an ideal weight. Excess weight is associated with a plethora of health risks, including diabetes, heart attack, and stroke. Even a few extra pounds can affect your ability to respond to stress, and your self-esteem.

3. Avoid fats. The typical American diet is 37 percent fat, which is too high and puts many people at risk.

4. Eat more whole foods. By eating foods such as raw or steamed vegetables, fruits, grains, rice, and cereals, you increase your consumption of fiber. Fiber is important for weight control and disease prevention.

5. Avoid sugar. Providing nothing but calories, sugar produces a quick "high," but subsequently blood sugar drops to a level lower than before the sugar was ingested. This roller-coaster effect is energy-depleting.

6. Use salt in moderation. Sodium is particularly hazardous to those with high blood pressure.

7. Use alcohol only in moderation. High in calories, alcohol depletes the body of B vitamins, which are important in coping with stress.

8. Use caffeine only in moderation. Caffeine induces the fight-or-flight response and inhibits the ability to cope with stress. It also depletes the body of vitamin B.

9. Use vitamin and mineral supplements. There is considerable controversy about the supplementation of diet. Stressed individuals require more of all vitamins and minerals, especially the B vitamins. Ornish recommends a multivitamin without iron.

10. Eat calm, frequent meals. Frequent meals prevent the stresses of being over-hungry and maintain more constant blood-sugar levels. Natural relaxation can be derived from nutritious foods eaten in a peaceful setting.

Positive personal habits

Cartwright and Cooper have come up with other ways to improve your physical well-being at work. These include arranging your physical work space for comfort and efficiency, working intensely using periodic sanity breaks for recovery, deep breathing on a periodic basis, and being normal rather than perfect by admitting your physical limitations. In addition, we recommend venting steam once in a while and getting enough sleep.

Restful sleep

The brain, which controls biological survival, needs rest to maintain its equilibrium. The brain, without adequate rest and sleep, cannot maintain the biochemical and electrical balances needed for effective functioning. When the brain is in a state of disequilibrium, a person cannot cope effectively (Quick *et al.*, 1997). Sleep disturbance affects both functioning and mood states and denies the body the opportunity for recuperation and repair. Difficulty falling asleep, insomnia, and early-morning awakening can all reflect depression or anxiety. Individuals who rely on alcohol to unwind and fall asleep in the evening may often find they awaken in the early morning when their bodies respond to an alcohol-induced adrenalin surge (Quick *et al.*, 1997). Individual differences in sleep patterns and needs vary greatly, but we recognize our own particular pattern of behavior and usually realize that changes may signal strain or pressure. A relaxation exercise, walking the dog, or taking a warm bath before retiring to bed may facilitate sleep. Part of our personal action plan for dealing with stress might include resolving to put aside emotional conflicts, or to avoid overeating in the evening hours. Daytime rest periods may also be beneficial. The break must involve a complete withdrawal from the day's activities, but even a brief change in scenery can be refreshing. Shaffer also suggests that daytime resting or breaks can moderate illness.

Alcohol and smoking

Though both alcohol consumption and cigarette smoking can have fatal consequences, there is at least one important distinction between the two. Alcohol, in the right amounts, has been found to extend life. Smoking, on the other hand, is harmful in any amount and in the end is the primary cause of death in half of its users.

A growing number of studies have documented the beneficial effects of moderate alcohol consumption (one or two drinks per day). Moderate alcohol consumption may be associated with a reduction of 30 percent to 40 percent in the risk of coronary heart disease. There is some indication that polyphenols, which have strong antioxidant properties, give red wine an additional protective effect. Clearly excess use of alcohol is destructive of physical, work-performance, and social functioning. High levels of alcohol, particularly in binges, is associated with increased risk for coronary heart disease. A combination of firm family support, medical management, counseling, and support groups such as Alcoholics Anonymous, is necessary to overcome alcohol addiction.

Cigarette smoking continues to decline for most age groups in the United States and most countries of western and northern Europe. The exception is among teenage girls, where rates increased in the last decade. Smoking cessation can often be achieved with various combinations of simple determination, behavior modification, nicotine-replacement products, and support groups.

Preventive health maintenance

In 1887 the American traveler and author Mark Twain observed of one of his characters that, "He had had much experience of physicians, and said, 'the only way to keep your health is to eat what you don't want, drink what you don't like, and do what you'd druther not.'"

Many busy executives are more conscientious and spend more time maintaining their Mercedes or their Range Rover than they do maintaining their own health. A car that may be traded in after only a few years and that can be replaced at any time is given more attention than one's own physical health, which must last a lifetime and can never be replaced.

A heart-healthy lifestyle, physical fitness, healthy eating habits, and healthy personal habits are all important parts of preventive health maintanence. Regular physical examinations and selective screening tests help to monitor risks factors and to detect cancer in its early stages. A growing number of cancers are treatable – some now curable – if caught early enough. While specific recommendations vary with respect to initiation and frequency of screening, there are clear benefits in testing for high blood pressure, blood lipid abnormalities, prostate cancer, colorectal cancer, breast cancer, cervical cancer, and several other treatable conditions.

The payoff:
effectiveness, well-being and longevity

Physical health is the foundation for longevity and overall well-being. We cannot change our genes, which can have a significant effect on the risk of illness and on our aging process. However, we can choose to identify and manage our cardiovascular risks, we can choose to exercise regularly, we can choose to maintain a reasonable body weight and healthy diet, and we can work toward restful sleep and moderate alcohol consumption. Executives from a variety of fields have found that maintaining physical health, including physical fitness and weight control, is possible within the hectic pace of organizational life. Far from taking time and energy, healthy habits can increase energy, increase productivity, and success.

Chapter 6 in a nutshell

1. Physical health is a cornerstone for executives' and managers' ability to perform well and achieve.

2. It is essential for executives to recognize and manage their cardiovascular risk factors, including hostility and work stress. Heart-healthy behavior is achievable and desirable.

3. Moderately strenous physical exercise on most days of the week brings substantial health and psychological benefits. Muscle flexibility and strength training are also important.

4. A proper diet and weight control is a central ingredient to insuring physical health and increasing longevity.

5. Complement the three keys to physical health with personal ways of enhancing physical health and efficiency.

7

Psychological well-being

[A] business will not be turned into a hobby merely because the owner finds it pleasurable; suffering has never been made a prerequisite to deductibility. "Success in business is largely obtained by pleasurable interest therein."

Wilson versus Eisner, 282 F. 38 (2d Cir. 1922),
US Federal tax court ruling concerning business tax deductions

Bodily vigor is good, and vigor of intellect is even better . . .

Theodore Roosevelt, U.S. President,
writing about ideas to build your life on, March 31, 1900

It is not the years in your life which are important, but the life in your years.

Abraham Lincoln, US President during the Civil War period

During June, 2001, the rising workplace costs of mental illness received attention in the United States and that was followed by the issues of psychological trauma related to the September 11 incident in New York City. However, executives should remember that psychological health and well-being are more commonly the human condition than are psychological disturbance and mental illness. Unfortunately, there is no question that when pressure exceeds an executive's ability to cope, he or she is in the stress arena, and ill health is just around the corner. Many incidences of stress-related illness come in the form of poor psychological well-being or mental illness. Thus, mental stress at work was the single biggest source of illness and subsequent sickness absence among managers, even ahead of minor or serious illness. It need not be this way. Take, for example, the experience of Winston Churchill, who battled depression and depressive symptoms throughout his life. He balanced these challenging experiences with a host of healthy habits that enabled him to win out over the black dog and live a life that made a very positive difference in the world. The emotional expressiveness in his intimate letters to his wife Clementine and his pastime of painting were among the positive psychological expressions that enabled him to experience psychological well-being.

Strategies for improving psychological well-being

There are numerous preventive health-management strategies that executives can use to improve their mental health and well-being. Two key objectives in enhancing psychological well-being for executives should be to combat workaholism and manage, or overcome, hostility. These range among enhanced self-awareness, calendar planning and time management, and managing your perception of events.

Self-awareness

In this section we will provide some aids and techniques to reduce stress levels, but it is our firm belief that any success in dealing with stress must begin with self-knowledge. It is important to understand how your high stress is created. For example, you need to know whether it stems from personal conflicts within you, from a need to create more balance in your life, or from sources beyond your immediate control. Many stress-management experts have criticized organizations for doing too little to reduce stress at work. All too often the blame is placed on the employee, who is encouraged to become stress-resistant or more able to cope with stress at work. This is relevant because it is important for the individual to understand that he or she is not necessarily at fault. False acceptance of blame is likely to lead to inappropriate coping strategies. For example, if you believe that you are the only person in the department who cannot cope with the workload, you might become unhappy, or you might consume more than the occasional drink to relax or unwind or help you get to sleep, until this behavior becomes a need. For most people, there is no one problem that must be solved; neither is there only one answer. Poor coping with stress usually involves many factors, including the individual's personality and coping strategies, life events encountered, and degree of social support.

While there are many things an individual cannot control, such as the loss of a loved one, many things most certainly can be managed or at least modified by the individual. Often, self-knowledge brings the awareness that an individual must alter his or her perceptions, behavior, lifestyle, or personal situation in order to cope effectively with stress.

Listed in Table 7.1 are some of the problems executives experience, together with a comparison of adaptive and maladaptive behaviors. It can be seen that maladaptive behavior is often associated with denial of a problem; it is avoided or ignored, and often becomes aggravated until the situation becomes chronic or acute.

In all the situations shown in Table 7.1, there is something that the individual can do to transform maladaptive behaviors, which are harmful to the person and those around him or her, into adaptive behaviors. For some people, the changes required may be simple ones, but each of these behaviors takes the basic source of the stress and solves it, sometimes temporarily and perhaps permanently. Therefore, it is necessary to recognize the problem. This is not always easy because we often obscure the real reasons behind our problems. We find respectable stressors to blame. For example, overwork is a safe reason to explain our change in behavior, because everyone is complaining (constantly tired, fatigued/unable to sleep properly, smoking more cigarettes). In reality, the stress of being passed over for promotion, the disappointment, and the thwarted ambition might be the real reasons for the stress, but these are much harder to admit to ourselves and others. This could be the real stressor, but of course it might also make it much harder to cope with the overwork situation. Rarely do we cope with just one situation in isolation. This is what Cooper and Kelly call the stress-chain, where one situation is linked to another.

To understand those incidents and series of related incidents during the working days, weeks, and months that cause you distress, it might help to keep a *stress diary*. This should provide you with information about the type of situation or person that causes you the most difficulty. An awareness of this should help you to develop an action plan to mini-

Table 7.1 Adaptive and maladaptive responses to executive health problems

Stress agent	Adaptive behavior	Maladaptive behavior
Overwork	Delegates some work	Accepts work overload with result that general performance deteriorates
Lack of awareness of a particular company policy	Finds out what policy is	Guesses inappropriately
Poor working relationship with colleague	Confronts issue with colleague and negotiates better relationship	Attacks colleague indirectly through third party
Underpromotion	Leaves organization for another	Loses confidence and becomes convinced of own inadequacy
Company versus family demands	Negotiates with boss more "family time" (e.g., less travel, shorter hours, etc.)	Blames company for family discontent
Role ambiguity	Seeks clarification with colleagues or superior	Withdraws from some aspects of work role

Source: Cooper, Cooper, Eaker, 1988.

mize or eliminate the stress factor, or at the very least, to alert you to when a stressful event (in your terms) is about to take place. At the end of each day, for two to four weeks, list all the incidents and the people involved that caused you distress during the working day. In addition, indicate the actions taken and what you feel, in retrospect, you should have done. It might also be helpful to monitor your response to the stressor. You can soon learn to recognize your own personal stress warning signals, such as headaches, stomach pains, muscle tension, depression, anxiety, or a strong desire to escape from a situation. Try to record:

● day of the week and time
● the incident (what happened)
● the people involved
● what you did
● your physical and/or emotional feelings
● what you should have done.

At the end of the time allotted, survey the incidents and people involved which caused you the most stress, and try to pinpoint particular types of events and specific people who consistently seem to be implicated in stressful work experiences. For example, were your stressors varied, or did they consistently group into a certain type of incident? Were they related to:

● home and work over-spill problems (conflicting demands)?

● your work role (clarity, responsibility)?

● overload, time pressures, etc.?

● relationships at work?

● organizational style (very competitive, non-supportive)?

Were specific people consistently implicated in the stressful situation, e.g., the boss, your colleagues, your subordinates, patients, spouse, partner, the family, etc.? Look through all the types of events and the specific people involved, and begin to make action plans for the future to deal with the problem area.

For example, if you consistently find you had difficulty in dealing with your boss when it came to deadlines, think about the alternative strategies open to you to cope with this type of situation and the particular personality of the boss involved. Each incident and/or relationship can be managed if you accurately identify the problem and systematically think through the options or alternative methods of coping. Each of the coping strategies should then be ranked in terms of their likelihood of success in achieving your objectives, primarily to minimize future stress and to accomplish your work-related tasks and goals. The objective is to devote a space of a few hours to analyzing specifically when, where, and why you feel tense or stressful. Periodically setting aside time to analyze the sources of stress and balance in your life can become a tremendously rewarding habit. In addition, becoming aware of your body's responses to stress and anxiety can begin to provide valuable clues to what's happening in your life. For some people, actual changes in home or work arrangements may be necessary; others may find that changes are needed in their behavior, e.g., they may need to learn to relax or to become more assertive. Of course, a person can always choose not to make any changes and to continue as usual and hope for the best. The person who refuses to make changes in his or her life is really choosing to endure the present situation rather than trying to improve things. Change and taking responsibility may be difficult, but the rewards, in terms of personal happiness and effectiveness, may be worth the effort involved.

Albrecht (1979) provides cameo descriptions of low-stress versus high-stress lifestyles among managers, although these patterns are typical for many occupational groups. In Table 7.2, it is possible to compare the differences between reasonable living patterns and destructive ways of high-stress living. The table shows that many elements of the low-stress lifestyle are ways of living based on common sense, such as eating well and using alcohol sparingly or not at all. Other elements, such as the development of escape routes or of a lifestyle with little role conflict, are more creative approaches.

> Each incident and/or relationship can be managed if you accurately identify the problem and systematically think through the options or alternative methods of coping.

Table 7.2 High- and low-stress lifestyle

Stressful lifestyle	Low-stress lifestyle
Individual experiences chronic unrelieved stress	Individual accepts "creative" stress for distinct periods of challenging activity
Becomes trapped in one or more continuing stressful situations; struggles with stressful interpersonal relationships (family, spouse, lover, boss, coworkers, etc.)	Has "escape routes" allowing occasional detachment and relaxation; asserts own rights and needs; negotiates low-stress relationships of mutual respect; selects friends carefully; establishes relationships that are nourishing and not harmful
Engages in distasteful, dull, toxic, or otherwise unpleasant and unrewarding work	Engages in challenging, satisfying, worthwhile work that offers intrinsic rewards for accomplishment
Experiences continual time stress; too much to be done in available time	Maintains a well-balanced and challenging workload; overloads and crises are balanced by "breather" periods
Worries about potentially unpleasant upcoming events	Balances threatening events with worthwhile goals and positive events to which to look forward
Has poor health habits, e.g., eating, smoking, liquor, lack of exercise, poor level of physical fitness; life activities are "lopsided" or unbalanced, e.g., preoccupied with one activity such as	Maintains high level of physical fitness, eats well, uses alcohol and tobacco not at all or sparingly; life activities are balanced; individual invests energies in a variety of activities (e.g., work, social activities,

work, social activity, making money, solitude, or physical exercise	recreation, solitude, cultural pursuits, family and close relationships), which, in the aggregate, bring feelings of satisfaction
Finds it difficult to just "have a good time," relax, and enjoy momentary activities; experiences sexual activities as unpleasant, unrewarding, or socially competitive (e.g., by manipulation, "one-upping")	Finds pleasure in simple activities, without feeling a need to justify playful behavior; enjoys a full and exuberant sex life, with honest expression of sexual appetite
Sees life as a serious, difficult situation; little sense of humor	Enjoys life, on the whole; can laugh at him/herself, has a well-developed and well-exercised sense of humor
Conforms to imprisoning, punishing social roles	Lives a relatively role-free life; is able to express natural needs, desires, and feelings without apology
Accepts high pressure of stressful situations passively; suffers in silence	Acts assertively to re-engineer pressure situations whenever possible; renegotiates impossible deadlines; avoids being placed in unnecessary pressure situations; manages time effectively

Source: Albrecht, 1979.

Managing your lifestyle

Once you have identified what is happening in your life at work or at home and how you want to live, there are several courses of action that may help either to remove/reduce stress or to enable you to cope more effectively with strain and pressure. This requires making changes which can seem overwhelming at first; however, as Cooper *et al.* suggest, stress is not some all-powerful force in your life that cannot be resisted. By keeping a stress diary, you will be able to see more clearly that stress situations can be altered, managed, or balanced with positive experiences; for example, by rewarding yourself with a relaxing weekend break when a difficult and threatening situation has been satisfactorily finalized. It is also necessary to consider why you might be resistant to change or might insist on clinging to old ways that seem safe but which are harmful in the long term. Often we can see other's mistakes more readily than our own, so observe someone close who seems to be suffering from stress and try and work out how that person could change and improve her or his situation. Why does he or she take on more and more work, instead of saying "No"?

Are you behaving in the same way? Unfortunately, depressed people tend to find it difficult to see options, so an outside observer might be willing and better able to offer alternative ways of behaving. We must avoid being inflexible to change and be more willing to try out new ways of behaving in order to reduce or minimize the consequences of stress.

The ability to get outside of one's own skin and give to others, to focus on other people, to experience altruism is a psychologically healthy aspect lifestyle management. Southwest Airlines chairman of the board Herb Kelleher has exemplified this psychologically healthy attitude for over 20 years in the airline industry. The most concrete illustration of this attitude is found in his and his employees' active support of the Ronald McDonald Houses in the airlines cities served. These houses are set up to provide food and shelter for the families of chronically ill children with cancer. While Herb and the south-westerners take their work of serving air passengers very seriously, they do not take themselves too seriously. Rather, they focus on the needs and well-being of others, not just themselves. They have found that in the giving, they also receive richly in a wide variety of ways.

Time management

Time, like money, is a limited resource that can be used to good or bad effect. Although it is possible to make more money, unfortunately you can't knit more time – there can be only 24 hours in a day. The inability to manage time effectively is often a major source of stress. Although self-imposed time pressure can stimulate action, constantly working under time pressures over which we perceive ourselves to have little or no control – situations that we experience as demanding action, yet allowing no time to think – are unlikely to result in good performance. Although we may blame others for wasting our time, the biggest culprit is usually ourselves. Four major time-wasters are procrastination, disorganization, confusion, and the inability to delegate. Targeted accomplishment and task completion are only two productive alternatives to time-wasters for the use of time. Restorative and energy recovery activities are central and important time activities for the healthy, successful executive. These restorative and energy recovery activities include pastimes, which can be very beneficial in the long run.

In 1915, as the First Lord of the Admiralty, Winston Churchill conceived the bold Dardanelles campaign. Had the campaign succeeded, the

British Navy could have tipped the balance and hastened the end of World War I. Instead, the admiral on the scene pulled back, perhaps minutes short of victory. Abandoned by the Prime Minister, villified by the press, and forced from the Admiralty, Churchill remained in the Cabinet, but with no power. In this failure, perhaps the darkest moment of his life, Churchill took up the "muse of painting." In his essay, "Painting as a pastime," Churchill describes the importance of taking time out from the stress of high-pressure responsibility:

Many remedies are suggested for the avoidance of worry and mental overstrain by persons who, over prolonged periods, have to bear exceptional responsibilities and discharge duties upon a very large scale. Some advise exercise, and others, repose. Some counsel travel, and others, retreat. Some praise solitude, and others, gaiety. No doubt all these may play their part according to the individual temperament. But the element which is constant and common in all of them is Change. Change is the master key. A man can wear out a particular part of his mind by continually using it and tiring it, just in the same way as he can wear out the elbows of his coats . . . but the tired parts of the mind can be rested and strengthened, not merely by rest, but by using other parts . . . It is only when new cells are called into activity, when new stars become the lords of the ascendant, that relief, repose, refreshment are afforded.

Other pastimes include a wide range of sporting activities, either active or passive. The former fall into the category of exercise while the latter fall into the category of spectator sports, which may or may not be relaxing. In either event, they are constructive alternatives to focused and targeted accomplishment.

Relaxation and recovery

Changing long-established behavior patterns requires major stress-reduction efforts that take time. Problems are not always simple, and rarely does a single answer exist. While you are investing the time and energy needed to sort out the stress factors in your life, in the meantime there is immediate relief available to you: relaxation. The purpose of relaxation training is to reduce the individual's arousal level and to bring about a calmer state of affairs from both psychological and physiological perspectives. Psychologically, successful relaxation results in enhanced feelings of well-being, peacefulness, a sense of control, and a reduction in felt tension and anxiety; physiologically, decrease in blood pressure, respiration, and heart rate should take place.

Some of the original research on the relaxation response as the natural counter to the stress response was pioneered by Benson, although the technique of progressive relaxation was developed by Dr Edmund Jacobson in the 1920s.

Techniques taught include various forms of meditation, autogenic training (a combination of muscle relaxation and meditation), breathing exercises, progressive muscle relaxation, self-hypnosis, mental imagery, and visualization. Carrington *et al.*, who incorporated meditation/relaxation techniques in a stress-control program developed for the New York Telephone Company, reported that the techniques are easily learned and have positive psychological and physical effects on work stress when practiced regularly.

The body needs time to relax and recuperate from the effects of everyday stress. Some people can dissipate stress, while others bury it deep within themselves; for the latter, life seems to be a series of crises. The chronically uptight person seems to meet even a small problem as if it were a critical incident, as if somehow his survival were in jeopardy. A sudden call to go and see the boss, a snag in a project schedule, a disagreement with a co-worker, or a problem with a teenage son or daughter all take on the same apparent magnitude for the uptight person. Such a person meets even the smallest problem situations with an unnecessarily intense reaction (Albrecht, 1979). This kind of stress can reflect itself in a variety of personally damaging behaviors, such as excessive coffee or tea consumption, cigarette-smoking, drug-taking, and so forth. Most people believe, for example, that the coffee break provides a useful stress-free breathing space, which it can. It also, however, provides the individual not with a relaxant, but with a further stimulant, which can adversely affect the biochemical balance in the body. There are a whole range of activities we do during the course of each day which feel right at the time but which can have detrimental effects in the short or medium term. Shaffer's description of common misguided attempts to relax can be found in his book, *Life After Stress*. For example:

- Smoking cigarettes is seen as a pick-me-up or social activity that also provides increased energy, but at the same time it causes indigestion and poor sleep.

- Drinking wine is a pausing social activity and muscle relaxant, but wine is also a depressant, and drains energy.

- Eating sugar or chocolate is seen as a pick-me-up, arousing, and a social pause, but sugar provides only empty calories and is nutritionally poor.

Relaxation can combat some of these adverse reactions. The positive bodily outcomes of deep relaxation as a means of coping with peak arousal situations can be found in Table 7.3. This is achieved by the deep relaxation technique. It is a simple technique, which anyone can practice. If you feel somewhat tense about the thought of adding such a technique to your daily life, we suggest you make a commitment to practice relaxation on a daily basis for one month before deciding whether you want to continue. Following this technique is a brief description of a shorter relaxation technique, which you may find helpful and more compatible with your lifestyle.

For optimal effectiveness, deep relaxation is best done once or twice a day. Do not relax too frequently because it can lead to lethargy, nor too long because it may cause hallucinations. Relaxation assists your body in energy recovery, restoration, distress avoidance, and the prevention of tension, fatigue, and anxiety build-up. The relaxation response has been elicited for centuries by Western people through their time-honored tradition of peaceful prayer and by Eastern people through their time-honored tradition of meditation.

Table 7.3 The stress response versus the relaxation response

Physiological indicator	Peak arousal	Deep relaxation
Adrenaline	More	Less
Respiration	Faster	Slower
Heart	Faster	Slower
Arteries	Constrict	Dilate
Blood pressure	Increase	Decrease
Metabolism	Faster	Slower
Muscle tension	Increase	Decrease
Stomach acid	More	Less
Blood sugar	More	Less
Insulin	More	Less
Cholesterol in blood	More	Less
Brain waves	Beta	Alpha or theta

Source: Benson and Stark, 1996.

Brief relaxation exercise

Once an executive learns to relax, brief relaxation exercises can take a maximum of ten minutes to practice and still be very restorative. The purpose of relaxation and brief relaxation exercises are to recover energy and lower stress or tension levels. The purpose is not to turn an executive off completely.

Five- to ten-minute exercise:

1. *Select a comfortable sitting or reclining position.*

2. *Close your eyes and think about a place that you have been before that represents your ideal place for physical and mental relaxation. (It should be a quiet environment, perhaps the seashore, the mountains, or your own back garden. If you can't think of an ideal relaxation place, then create one in your mind.)*

3. *Now imagine that you are actually in your ideal relaxation place. Imagine that you are seeing all the colors, hearing the sounds, smelling the aromas. Just lie back, and enjoy your soothing, rejuvenating environment.*

4. *Feel the peacefulness, the calmness, and imagine your whole body and mind being renewed and refreshed.*

5. *After five to ten minutes, slowly open your eyes and stretch. You now have the knowledge that you may instantly return to your relaxation place whenever you desire, and experience a peacefulness and calmness in the body and mind.*

Managing your perceptions of events

The previously discussed methods of stress management are all aimed at building your stress resiliency and/or lowering your reactivity to stressful events. This section presents a more positive psychology by examining ways of lowering your reactions to stressful events by managing your perceptions of daily events. As we discussed in earlier chapters, the way an individual perceives a situation dramatically affects the stress response experienced. For example, Type-A individuals continually set off their stress responses by perceiving life as competitive and time-oriented. People who have an external locus of control perceive that they have little control over the situations that confront them daily. In contrast, the hardy personality perceives that he or she has a great deal of control of his or her life. In the last two cases, it is not so much the actual ability to cope with a situation as the individual's perception of his ability to cope that matters. Other research has shown that coping style is mediated by personality and associated with various health and disease outcomes. For example, in the management of diabetes, Cox has described the association between personality type and behavioral tendency: "Introverted diabetics tend to be more careful in balancing food intake to match insulin administration, and are more careful in maintaining sterile precautions." Furthermore, they appear more able to regulate their general lifestyle according to the requirements of the disorder. Extroverted diabetics, on the other hand, tend to hold more "easy-going" attitudes toward the disorder and tend, partly as a result, to underestimate the importance of careful dieting and to be less concerned about the accuracy and timing of their insulin injections. A number of reports in the literature describe cancer patients as repressive (Bahnson, 1981; Dattore *et al.*, 1980).

> People who have an external locus of control perceive that they have little control over the situations that confront them daily. In contrast, the hardy personality perceives that he or she has a great deal of control of his or her life.

Thus, the perception of events and/or coping styles may influence the onset or course of an illness and, conversely, help ameliorate and prevent the same. Several techniques are available to help in the cognitive reappraisal of stressful situations:

1. *Constructive self-talk* is described as intermittent mental monologue that most people conduct about the events they experience and their reactions to these events. This monologue or self-talk can range from being gently positive to harshly condemning. When someone engages in negative self-talk, they achieve nothing and just maintain the stress, dissipating their emotional energy. If you are involved in constructive self-talk, it can achieve more positive psychological results. A range of examples of situations, mental monologues and alternative

strategies for positive, constructive self-talk are shown in Table 7.4.

2. *Quick recovery* is the ability to bounce back from upsetting experiences. Learning to recover quickly takes little more than an awareness of how you actually do recover. As Albrecht describes it, once you begin to think about your emotional responses, you can recognize the process of returning to emotional equilibrium after a provocation has passed. For example, if you find yourself drawn into a personal confrontation, you will very likely experience anger and a full-blown stress response. Your higher-level mental processes will probably not be functioning very well, Albrecht explains. At a certain point, however, your emotions will begin to subside, and you will realize that you are angry. That is, you will experience your anger as an intellectual concept as well as a physical feeling. Albrecht states that at this point, you have the option, on the one hand, to continue to aggravate your angry feelings by rehashing the provocation, rejustifying your position, reopening a new attack on your adversaries, and becoming newly outraged by their unreasonable behavior. On the other hand, a quick recovery approach would suggest that you stop this negative circular approach and become more rational and less conscious of your need to win.

3. *Thought stopping* means recognizing non-constructive thoughts, attitudes, and behaviors and stopping them immediately by visualizing, for example, a large STOP sign. Then turn the corner and develop some positive and constructive thoughts.

4. *Mental diversion* diverts the topic, issue, or crisis to one that is manageable, until one has resources to cope with it. As Quick and Quick suggest, one way to stop a thought pattern is to divert yourself to a more positive topic. For instance, once you have prepared yourself adequately for the coming event, such as a presentation or interview, obsessive worry can only drain your emotional resources. Diverting your thoughts to a more pleasant, restful subject can stop a negative thought pattern.

Table 7.4 Constructive self-talk

Situation	Typical Mental Monologue	Constructive self-talk alternative
Driving to work on a day which you know will be full of appointments and potentially stressful meetings	Oh boy, what a day this will be! It's going to be hell! I'll never get it all done It'll be exhausting	This looks like a busy day The day should be very productive I'll get a lot accomplished today I'll earn a good night's rest today
Anticipation of a seminar presentation or public address	What if I blow it? Nobody will laugh at my opening joke What if they ask about . . .? I hate talking to groups	This ought to be a challenge I'll take a deep breath and relax They'll enjoy it Each presentation goes a bit better
Recovering from a heart attack	I almost died I'll die soon I'll never be able to work again I'll never be able to play sports again	I didn't die. I made it through The doctor says I'll be able to get back to work soon I can keep active and gradually get back to most of my old sports
Difficulty with a superior at work	I hate that person! He makes me feel stupid We'll never get along	I don't feel comfortable with him I let myself get on edge It will take some effort to get along
Flat tire on a business trip	Damn this old car! (Paces around car, looking at flat tire) I'll miss all my meetings It's hopeless	Bad time for a flat (Begins to get tools out to start working) I'll call and cancel Jenkins at the next phone I should make the rest of my appointments

Emotional expression and venting

The ability to express emotions and feelings naturally are central to psychological well-being. Emotional expression can take on a variety of forms. Winston Churchill and Abigail Adams, wife of US President John Adams, both used writing letters to their spouses as an essential means of emotional expression. US President Harry Truman was known to write scathing letters to the editors of print publications that were critical of either his wife or his daughter. However, it was not uncommon for the letter never to arrive at its destination but rather for it to see the circular file. The president has expressed himself and yet not done damage to an otherwise good professional relationship. Truman's letter writing was a form of venting.

The venting of emotions may occur through humor and jokes, but ones which are not done at the expense of another person. For example, when Herb Kelleher presented the 1990 Distinguished Business Leadership Award to American Airlines President Bob Crandall, he infused the evening with humor (Quick, 1992, p. 49):

Bob, it is a real pleasure to be here tonight to present you with this award. True, it would be an even more delightful evening if you were presenting me with this award. But . . . I can forgive the dean his error in judgment.

Diary-writing and humor are two means of emotional expression for psychological well-being. A quick wit may be combined with song to create a positive response within a professional setting. Ebby Halliday, the entrepreneur who pioneered one of the largest privately owned residential real-estate companies in the US, used song to help lift her own spirits and those of her colleagues during a challenging meeting about the difficulties in the Texas real-estate industry during the 1980s. After a serious address during the early stages of recovery in the industry, Ebby Halliday proceeded to bring out her ukelele and deliver the following performance to the tune of "Happy Days Are Here Again" (Quick, Nelson, Quick, 1990, p. 112):

Happy days are here again,
Interest rates are down again
Builders build and realtors wear a grin
Happy days are here again.

Even though oil price is down
Other business can always be found
Roll up your sleeves – there's always work to do
Sell pre-owned homes as well as new
Then there's land and lots and commercial, too
Happy days are here again!

Even anger can be expressed in a healthy way so that people, objects, and feelings are not unnecessarily hurt or injured. While hostility is lethal for the heart, the experience and then expression of anger in appropriate ways releases the executive from the burden of harbored hostility.

Seeking social support

In addition to the various self-help activities described, it is also important to find the social support that you need. Research has found that social support functions as a strong buffer against the stresses of work and life generally. A major source of support can be found among family members and friends, but social support and friendships developed at work can also be extremely valuable.

Support within the family

In most cases, the workplace creates a greater proportion of stress compared to the home environment. Much of this workplace stress, however, spills over to adversely affect our partners and families. Changes in society also combine to put pressures and strains into family life. To minimize these problems and to avoid the vicious spiral of stress, the family must work as a unit. According to Shaffer, effective communication in the family unit is the first vital step in providing the foundation for an atmosphere of trust and openness. He advises that family members should speak clearly, each to one another, check out and clarify meanings, and ensure that the messages have been understood. In order to develop a closely bonded unit that is able to deal with problems, all members of the family must be involved in the adoption of strategies which negotiate the issues of roles, boundaries, and conflicts. This should not be a vague session in which the individual members explode or are critical of the lack of family support, but rather a constructive, detailed and concise review of the conflict, time commitments, role confusion or anything else that is undermining the cohesiveness of the family. The conversation should conclude by developing an action plan that distributes tasks among family members, resolves some conflict, or

> In order to develop a closely bonded unit that is able to deal with problems, all members of the family must be involved in the adoption of strategies which negotiate the issues of roles, boundaries, and conflicts.

in some other way follows through to resolution a significant issue for the family or one of its members. For example, if there are problems concerning time commitment and/or role among family members, the following role-negotiation strategy could be followed (Cooper *et al.*, 1988):

1. Prepare a balance sheet of work and home commitments, listing details of hours spent, tasks undertaken, etc.

2. Call a formal family meeting to share concerns and discuss the detailed balance sheet.

3. Renegotiate various family commitments.

4. Create mutual action plans that are agreed by all family members for the next three months.

5. Review the success, or otherwise, of action plans at the end of a three-month period.

6. Develop new action plans based on the experience of the previous ones. Continue the process until all parties are adequately satisfied with arrangements.

The family can provide excellent support and a haven against the pressures and strains of work. A non-supportive family environment, however, creates a double jeopardy for the individual who also works in a stressful job.

Support at work

In addition to strengthening family ties, individuals can seek support at work. One of the most important sources of social support may be found through the informal work group. The complicated sets of relationships at work and their potential for conflict and ambiguity make it necessary for individuals to seek support from their peers. In this respect, Cooper *et al.* suggest a number of different approaches one can take. First, those responsible for people within organizations should create the right atmosphere to encourage social-support networks and to provide the most appropriate resources for stress management. Second, the individual can act to create these networks. Below are a number of steps an individual under stress may take to find social support at work:

1. Choose someone at work you feel you can talk to, someone you don't feel threatened by and to whom you can trustfully reveal your feelings. For the purpose of this exercise, avoid people who,

on reflection, you may be using on an unconscious level as pawns in a game of organizational politics, in itself a strategy you might do well to re-evaluate!

2. Approach this person and explain that you have a particular problem at work or outside work that you would like to discuss. Admit that you need help and that he or she would be the best person to consult because you trust his or her opinion, like him or her as a person, and feel that he or she can usefully identify with your circumstances.

3. Try to maintain and build on this relationship, even at times free of crisis or problem.

4. Review, from time to time, the nature of the relationship, to see if it is still providing you with the emotional support you need in order to cope with the difficulties that arise. If the relationship is no longer constructive or the nature of your problems have changed (requiring a different peer counsellor), then seek another person for support.

Often, the individual feels that the boss or supervisor does not provide the needed support at work. If this is a problem perceived by the work group or team it could be tackled at this level. Being more assertive about one's needs and expectations is a potentially difficult situation in such circumstances, but the use of open communication patterns and a willingness to change or negotiate can help to improve the social climate at work. It is important for those of us in need of help to own up to our difficulties and not to rely totally on the organization always to be available and competent to resolve them. We must take personal initiatives to seek the kind of professional or peer help that may be necessary, if pressure is experienced at work and we feel unable adequately to cope alone.

Chapter 7 in a nutshell

1. Self-awareness is the first step in positive psychological well-being.

2. Lifestyle management and balance between work and personal life enhance mental health.

3. Time management for both targeted achievement and pastimes is a key to balance and health.

4. Relaxation can be achieved in many ways, including prayer and meditation.

5. Managing your perceptions and expressing your emotions in healthy ways enhances psychological well-being.

8

Spiritual vitality

How prompt we are to satisfy the hunger and thirst of our bodies; how slow to satisfy the hunger and thirst of our souls!

Henry David Thoreau, 1853

I believe that forgiving them is God's function.
Our job is simply to arrange the meeting.

General (retired) Norman Schwartzkopf when asked if there was room for forgiving those who harbored and abetted the terrorists who perpetrated the September 11 attacks on America.

The last half of the twentieth century brought about much change in the way we approach our personal as well as our professional lives. In the 1950s most businessmen dreamed of the house in the suburbs with a stay-at-home wife, 3.4 children, and a career that included one long-term position. Today the dream and the reality have changed. Men and women enter the workforce in almost equal numbers. Their dreams of the future often include a spouse with a career at least as important and demanding as their own. If children are a part of the dream, the number desired has decreased to 1.2, and sometimes the house in the suburbs is a high-rise condo in the heart of town.

> We believe the missing piece in so many lives is a fulfillment of a higher order, a cultivation and development of the soul. In other words, we believe this missing piece is a personal and professional life of spirituality.

While this new dream has fulfilled many of our material and financial desires, it has left many people with a feeling of emptiness. They have achieved everything they had ever thought they wanted, but somehow they continue to feel less than fulfilled. This emptiness has left many wondering what they have missed. We believe the missing piece in so many lives is a fulfillment of a higher order, a cultivation and development of the soul. In other words, we believe this missing piece is a personal and professional life of spirituality.

Sound leaders

As outlined in earlier chapters of this book, a manager must first ensure his or her physical health. It is upon this foundation that all other aspects of health can be built. While a manager or executive may think that addressing other needs is more urgent, if his or her health is not good, there is no guarantee that he or she will continue in the leadership position. The time taken away from work to address essential health needs, such as exercise and diet, are well worth the investment. Attention to these issues will enhance the manager's ability to do a good job of leading the organization.

Once the manager's or executive's health is ensured, he or she can focus on building psychological health. The ability to see reality clearly is critical to a leadership position. A leader sets the psychological tone for the entire organization. If the leader is suspicious and paranoid, the organization will follow suit. If the leader is stable, the organization will follow this lead also.

Without both physical and psychological health secured, it is difficult, if not impossible, to build one's spirituality. Spirituality has no single definition. It is described in different ways by different people. In researching *A Spiritual Audit of Corporate America*, Ian Mitroff and Elizabeth Denton spoke with many individuals about the meaning of spirituality. In collecting this information, several ideas were offered repeatedly. In general, these ideas stated that spirituality is a highly individual and intensely personal issue. It is the basic belief that there is a supreme power. Spirituality is believing that everything is interconnected, and it is the feeling of this interconnectedness. It is believing that no matter how bad things get, they will work out, and that we are put here to do good. And finally, spirituality is inextricably connected with caring, hope, kindness, love, and optimism.

Using these responses to the meaning of spirituality, Mitroff and Denton developed a definition of the concept that includes what it is:

broadly inclusive, universal, timeless, and the ultimate source and provider of meaning and purpose in life. The definition also includes what spirituality is not. It is not denominational, and in contrast to conventional religion, it is neither formal, structured, nor organized. Spirituality is a deep feeling of connectedness with everything, an inner peace and calm, and an inexhaustible source of faith and willpower that is important to every aspect of our lives.

Adding a sense of fulfillment and spiritual vitality adds depth to an executive's life. It allows him or her to look beyond the day-to-day tasks of life and see a greater purpose or goal. Spirituality allows the manager or executive not only to recognize this added dimension to his or her own personal life, but also to bring this insight to the organization. A spiritually alive manager can lead the organization to a spiritual awakening that will improve the lives of everyone involved.

Sound organizations

There are three basic functions of any business organization: to produce, to consume, and to defend. No matter what type of organization, whether manufacturing or service, it must produce, consume, and defend to remain a viable entity. The first task of the organization is to produce its product or service. It must produce a product that has quality and value. Next the organization must market and sell this product to consumers. It must sell it at a price that is low enough to be acceptable to the consumer while still providing sufficient capital to the organization to pay its bills and produce a normal profit. And finally, the organization must defend itself against competitors who want to lure away its customers.

These functions are imperative for any organization to survive. But just like the individual, successfully producing, consuming, and defending may leave an organization hollow and lacking fulfillment. A spiritually vital leader can engage and energize an organization to achieve a feeling of fulfillment as a community. A spiritually vital organization goes way beyond its three primary functions. It gives back to its members and to the community in which it operates. It allows everyone to profit from its existence.

Mitroff and Denton offer several models of spirituality for corporate organizations. The first model is the "religion-based organization". While this model is the most extreme in terms of developing spirituality in the workplace, it offers a template for those individuals who start an organization fundamentally grounded in a particular religion and its beliefs. While this type of organization is ideal for religion-based organizations such as churches, synagogues or mosques, this model offers little for secular corporations. The next two models are the "evolutionary organization" and the "recovering organization". Both of these models are only slightly more traditional than the religion-based organization.

The evolutionary organization is an organization that has evolved beyond the religion-based to develop a mission that is more secular. The YMCA is a perfect example of such an organization. The YMCA was originally formed to be a protestant Christian organization to help individuals who were migrating from the farm to urban areas. It was a place where these individuals could live, eat, and worship to avoid the evil lures of the city. Since its inception, the mission of the YMCA has become more diverse than merely providing a Christian haven for immigrants to the city.

The recovering organization tends to be somewhat extreme in its views also. It is often led by key executives who are in recovery from addictions to things such as alcohol or gambling and who adopt the management principles of recovery programs. The principles of programs such as Alcoholics Anonymous become the guiding principles of the organization. The spiritual nature of this organization is in everyone's commitment to the guiding principles and the embodiment of spirituality within them. This organization embraces the spirituality that stems from commitment to its guiding principles but tends not to foster any other types of spirituality.

The fourth model of a spiritual organization is the "values-based organization". General philosophical principles or values guide this organization. It is not aligned with a religion nor does it directly speak to spirituality; however, there is an underlying, implicit definition of spirituality in these organizations. The last model offered by Mitroff and Denton is the "socially responsible organization". This organization is typically founded by a person who has strong spiritual principles or values that they apply to the business. These leaders have a strong commitment not only to the internal members of the organization but also to their outside stakeholders.

Andrew Carnegie

One of the greatest historical examples of a spiritually vital executive who created a socially responsible organization is Andrew Carnegie. Carnegie was the first-born son of a poor family from Scotland. At age twelve, Carnegie emigrated to the United States with his father, mother and younger brother. His father had trouble finding work after moving to Pennsylvania (Hacker, 1968). Giving up his search for work, he supported his family by weaving cloth at home and peddling his wares door to door. Even with his mother's strict management of the family, it was necessary for Carnegie to work at a cotton mill as a bobbin boy for $1.20 per week.

Carnegie adapted quickly to America. He marveled at the opportunities that America offered everyone. Unlike the rigid class system of the United Kingdom, hard work in this new country could make anyone a financial success. Carnegie was determined to make it work for him. From 1856, when Carnegie received his first dividend check for $5, until 1902, when J. P. Morgan purchased Carnegie Steel for $480 million, he was busy making money. However, money was never an end in itself for Carnegie. Money was simply a means to an end for himself, his family, friends, and community.

In June of 1889, the *North American Review* published his article called "Wealth," to which there was an editorial reply in December of 1889 in which the term "the gospel of wealth" was first used. Carnegie defended great wealth as an inevitable outcome of the capitalist system. He also claimed it was beneficial, provided that the amasser of the wealth realized that he or she was but a steward responsible for returning that fortune to the society out of which it came. In his "Wealth" article, Carnegie describes four of his many philanthropic endeavors. The first was the library gifts, the best known and most widely acclaimed of all his benefactions. The three other endowments are the Andrew Carnegie Relief Fund, established in 1901 to provide financial assistance for his employees in need; the Carnegie Institution of Washington, which provides the funds to encourage investigations, research and discovery; and the Carnegie Hero Fund, a pension fund for heroes who were disabled or for support of families of those who died in a heroic act. In total, through these four funds combined with numerous others, Andrew Carnegie gave away over $350 million during his lifetime (Wall, 1992).

Spirituality versus religion

We want to emphasize that what we are talking about is spirituality, not religion. Religion is inappropriate for the workplace. Religion is a structured belief system that addresses universal spiritual questions and provides a framework for making sense out of our existence. It is organized and expects general adherence to a particular body of beliefs. Each of us has the right to practice our own personal religious beliefs in whatever religious denomination we choose. We also have the right to the privacy of that faith and to be free from persecution or ridicule in the workplace. However, this privacy of personal religious choices does not preclude the right to work in a spiritually alive and vibrant environment.

Spirituality, on the other hand, is a broader idea that relates to issues of purpose, hope, and relationships. Spirituality allows people of all denominations to work together to create an organization that is united in its belief in a greater meaning to their lives at work. A spiritually alive organization enables the members to feel that their day at work contributes more than just accomplishing tasks and earning financial compensation. Spiritual organizations offer members an opportunity to feel that they are contributing to a greater good and a higher purpose. It allows people to rise above the needs of self and to contribute beyond their personal gain.

> A spiritually alive organization enables the members to feel that their day at work contributes more than just accomplishing tasks and earning financial compensation.

To some degree, we all work for the financial compensations that accompany employment. Many of us attain a level of professional achievement that affords us a wonderful life. Sometimes an individual's achievement rises to such a level where he or she has attained more financial success than is imaginable. These individuals enjoy such financial success that they not only need nothing, they want for nothing. They have everything and anything that financial success can buy; yet they still find no contentment in their lives. One such example is John D. Rockefeller. Rockefeller offers us a man who saved his own life when he realized that financial success alone offered little in the long run.

John D. Rockefeller

An examination of the early life of John D. Rockefeller offers an example of a man whose only passion in life was making money and protecting that money for himself. Unlike Carnegie, Rockefeller desired the money as an end in itself. He wasn't concerned with his family, friends, or community. All he wanted was to make more and more money and to hoard every penny of it. That was the way John D. Rockefeller Sr was, at least for the first part of his life.

By the age of 53, Rockefeller was on the verge of death. He was being attacked by a mysterious digestive problem. Rockefeller had lost a lot of weight, lost all of his hair, including his eyebrows and eyelashes, and all the doctors would allow him to eat was a few crackers and some acidulated milk. He could not stand up straight. What was causing a relatively young man to suffer these life-threatening maladies? A life of worry and tension was at the root of Rockefeller's health problems.

Rockefeller was already totally absorbed with earning money by the early age of 23. His demeanor was always grim, except when he was taking advantage of a bargain and earning more money. Every night Rockefeller went to bed and worried about losing his money. The worry of losing his money was always present. Even at a time when his company was doing a gross business of $500,000 a year, Rockefeller was so distraught over losing $150 that he was unable to get out of bed for two days.

Rockefeller claimed that he wanted to be loved, yet his love of money drove him to do things that made people despise him. The men working for Standard Oil Company hated him, filling his office with letters so threatening that Rockefeller hired bodyguards for his protection. Other millionaires, like J. P. Morgan, disliked him so much that they didn't want to do business with him unless there was no other alternative. Even his own brother hated him so much he refused to allow any member of his family to be buried in the same cemetery plot as John.

Although Rockefeller tried to ignore all this hatred, he was unable to. This, combined with the worry over losing his money, is what put him in the physical condition he was in by age 53. It was at this point that the doctors told John that he must stop worrying and relax, or he was going to die. Rockefeller took this advice to heart and turned his life around. During his recovery he began to reflect on his life and his treatment of others. He began to realize that all the money he had accumulated had never brought him real happiness. It was at this point that Rockefeller began to give his millions away.

While many benefited from the generosity of John D. Rockefeller, no one benefited more than Rockefeller himself. He realized in mid-life that his love of money was destroying him. It took years of worry, greed, and being hated for him to realize that there was more to life than money.

Milton Hershey

Although it took Rockefeller over 50 years to come to these realizations, other people have started their professional careers recognizing the importance of building an organization that provides not only financial benefits to the owner and the workers but also offers all a fuller, richer experience. One of the most enduring examples of this type of executive is Milton Hershey. From the very beginning, Hershey's concern was for the well-being of everyone involved in his organization.

At the turn of the century, Hershey built a company that would grow to be one of the most enduring examples of a spiritually vital and socially responsible organization. He also built a community around that company, so all could share in his dream and success. In addition to the business complex, Hershey built a town with all of the accoutrements of a large city. The town of Hershey, Pennsylvania, was complete with the Hershey hospital, theater, park, college, and orphanage. But what really makes the story of Milton Hershey important is his strength of character in the face of the Great Depression.

Although the revenue of the company plummeted to a low of $21 million in 1933, half of its 1929 peak, Hershey made sure that his townspeople didn't suffer. He maintained the rigid production schedule, cutting no wages and discharging no employees. Instead, in the face of these difficult times, he fought the Great Depression with his own building campaign, spending more than $10 million on improving the city, adding attractions to the town to draw tourists, and expanding the factory to add more jobs. Milton Hershey placed the future of the people and the town above his own financial security.

Both Rockefeller and Hershey were building their empires during the turn of the century, when their entrepreneurial spirits and hard work produced the success they enjoyed. Their ability to spend their respective fortunes did not receive the scrutiny of mass media or a board of directors, as many corporations today must face. Today's executive must face many challenges when deciding the direction of his or her company. In making the commitment to develop an organization that meets the spiritual needs of the employees and the community, he or she must recognize that this commitment may cause challenges for the business not faced by competitors. The case of Truett Cathy and Chick-fil-A is an example of an organization successfully competing while keeping its commitment to a spiritual existence.

Truett Cathy

When you think of the big fast-food restaurant chains, usually what comes to mind is McDonald's, Wendy's, and Kentucky Fried Chicken. When you think of the fast-food business leaders, names like Ray Kroc, R. David Thomas, and Colonel Sanders crop up. There is, however, a new story being written about an emerging titan in the land of the fast-food giants. The company is Chick-fil-A and the founder is Truett Cathy. What makes this story unique is that the company is privately held, as well as its blend of spirituality and business acumen.

Currently, this company has over nine hundred restaurants operating in 34 states and South Africa. Sales are over $1 billion annually.

What makes this success even more amazing is that these sales are achieved in only six days instead of the usual seven days of other fast-food chains. The decision to close on Sundays was made over 50 years ago and continues to this day. It is not an option for the restaurants, but a mandatory operating standard. For most restaurants, Sunday sales represent 20 percent of their total sales volume, and closing Sundays would mean that they could not remain in business.

The reason that Chick-fil-A closes on Sunday has to do with its spiritual commitments. Mr Cathy believes that his employees should spend Sunday with their families, going to church services, and getting much needed rest. He believes that the business prospers because such a decision leads to a more loyal and happier employee. Chick-fil-A has one of the lowest turnover rates among its independent owner–operators, at 4 percent, in the entire restaurant industry.

Truett Cathy is known as a devoutly religious man who believes that hard work, biblical principle, and service to humanity are the cornerstones to success in life and business. This is very evident in the mission statement of the Chick-fil-A organization: "To glorify God by being a faithful steward of all that is entrusted to us. To have a positive influence on all who come in contact with Chick-fil-A." In addition to closing on Sunday, further evidence of these beliefs comes from his support of education. Beginning in 1973, the company has awarded more than $14.6 million in scholarships. In 1999, the company gave out scholarships totaling $993,000.

Another noteworthy program that Mr Cathy supports concerns children. Beginning with a visit to Berry College, located in Rome, Georgia, in 1982, Cathy formed a plan to help less-fortunate children. First, he created an institution called the WinShape Centre. The focus of the Win-Shape Centre was a facility for Chick-fil-A scholarship awardees, a boys and girls summer camp, and a foster home. Next, he set up the Win-Shape Foundation with Chick-fil-A as the primary benefactor. In 1984, 68 students enrolled in the WinShape Centre, and in 1997, 120 students were admitted. These students are awarded $10,000 per year in the first year of college and a lesser amount each year thereafter. This follows Mr

Cathy's belief in hard work whereby students are encouraged to work to pay for part of their college educations.

The Centre started the boys' summer camp in the summer of 1985. The girls' summer camp began in 1987. Activities keep the camp attendees, ages seven through 16, busy from dawn to dusk. From modest enrollment in the initial years, current enrollment is over 1,500.

The WinShape Homes program provides homes to less-fortunate children. Starting with one 5,000 ft^2 home, there are now 11 WinShape Homes. Each home has a married couple, to provide a home environment and to serve as role models, and 12 children. The concept is to help each child from the time they enter the program until well beyond their 18th birthday. The focus is to get the child ready for his or her chosen career.

Benefits to the world of spiritually vital executives

The inspirational individuals we have discussed so far in this chapter demonstrate that when executives realize the impact they and their organizations can have beyond the primary function of business, everyone benefits. However, these individuals are by far not the only examples history has to offer us in the way of spiritually alive managers and executives. More and more we hear stories of men and women using their leadership positions and their visibility to promote causes near and dear to their hearts. The following are examples of some of those individuals using their money and influence to make the world a better place.

> More and more we hear stories of men and women using their leadership positions and their visibility to promote causes near and dear to their hearts.

R. David Thomas

Everyone knew the late R. David Thomas as the founder of Wendy's International and the father of the chain's namesake: Wendy. By any standard, he was a very successful businessman. He was also the spokesman for those very memorable Wendy's commercials. As successful as he was in the restaurant business, there are two other reasons why R. David Thomas is famous. The first is adoption and the second is education. What is interesting to note is that both of these causes had very special meaning for Mr Thomas.

Adoption was important to Mr Thomas because he himself was adopted as a baby. He did not discover this fact until he was thirteen, and the news had a profound affect on him. He reacted angrily and was hurt by the fact that his family waited so long to tell him. Although he was grateful to have been adopted and not left as a ward of the state, he wanted to meet and know his biological parents. Decades later, when President Bush asked Mr Thomas to do something for children waiting for adoption, he took the request as a personal challenge. He created a program that gives Wendy's employees adoption benefits including financial aid and paid time off for adoption-related issues. In addition to this program, he has contacted the heads of America's 1,000 largest companies urging them to do the same.

The other cause that had special meaning for Mr Thomas is education. He quit school after the tenth grade because he knew he wanted to be a restauranteur, and he felt that school was not providing the training he needed for that vocation. However, he appreciates the value of an education in today's world and does all he can to encourage young people to complete their educations.

As evidence of his support of education, he made a substantial financial contribution to Duke University. In turn, the university built the R. David Thomas Center that is part of the Fuqua School of Business. The R. David Thomas Center provides executive education for managers from various fields.

John Templeton

Sir John Marks Templeton's 45-year career on Wall Street could be defined by three characteristics: humility, contrarianism, and incredible success. It was humility that gave him insights into his customers' needs. Realizing that they desire a good financial return but are unwilling to gamble their hard-earned money on one or two stocks, he began investing on an international scale. This also caused him to be known as a contrarian, because his methods ran against the prevailing wisdom of his day. His investing strategies did, however, prove to be very successful, growing at a rate of 15 percent per year over the course of 45 years.

During the early years of his career, Templeton was recruited to sit on the board of Princeton Theological Seminary, and later he became its chairman. From this vantage point, he compared the progress made in religious thinking with scientific advances. He saw that there was a serious gap between the two. During his 30 years on the board, he became acutely aware of how few new ideas were presented. It was as if religion was static, and the premise was that all answers were already provided, so new thinking was discouraged.

To encourage advancement in religious thinking, Mr Templeton set up the Templeton Prize in 1972. The annual award of $1 million would go to the person making the most substantial innovative contribution in religion. The first recipient of the prize was Mother Teresa. Her contribution was for loving the dying. She spent the greater portion of her life providing for the needs of the dying in some of the poorest countries on earth.

Sir John Templeton created the John Templeton Foundation in 1987 to promote the importance of the moral and spiritual dimensions of life. The Templeton Foundation supports studies in these areas. Currently, there are more than 150 projects, studies, awards programs, and publications worldwide.

The Templeton Foundation Press was founded in 1997 to publish scholarly and trade books on topics such as the connection between science and religion, spiritual healing in medicine, universal spiritual laws, and character development. Templeton's book (1997) *The Worldwide Laws of Life* grew out of his belief that spiritual wisdom exists not only in religious teaching but also in the wisdom of many cultures, such as found in ordinary folk sayings. To accomplish the compilation of these sayings, he funded a group of scholars to collect them. The result is a collection of 200 maxims that feature timeless principles that lead to a developed character.

Four decades after he won a Rhodes scholarship to Oxford, Sir John Templeton returned the favor by building Templeton College, a business school at Oxford. Another project at Oxford supported by the Foundation is the John Templeton Oxford Seminars on Science and Christianity. The seminars seek to bring together the best scholars from the United States and Britain in the areas of religion, science, and philosophy. The focus of the seminars is to encourage young faculty members to conduct scholarly research in this field. This reflects the John Templeton Foundation's aim to bring together the religious and scientific communities to create a scholarly relationship between the two fields.

Bill Gates

If you have ever used a computer, then you have probably heard of Bill Gates. He is one of the founders and the driving force behind Microsoft Corporation. Mr Gates is well known for his aggressive approach to business and for a very strongly competitive nature.

Bill Gates is also making a name for himself in the philanthropic world. Together with his wife, he has established the William and Melinda Gates Foundation. This foundation is actually the result of combining their three foundations into one. The William and Melinda Gates Foundation absorbed the Gates Learning Foundation and the William H. Gates Foundation. What makes this resulting foundation so newsworthy is the size of the gifts awarded by Bill and Melinda Gates. To date, they have given $21.8 billion, making this the largest foundation in history.

Mr Gates seems to be following in the footsteps of his parents. Both were very active in charitable organizations. In fact, his father, William H. Gates Sr, served as a United Way national board member. His mother, also a leader in the United Way, is often credited with having a strong influence on her son's philanthropy.

Mr Gates is also following the blueprint provided by other business giants such as John D. Rockefeller, Andrew Carnegie, Henry Ford, and David Packard. Creating their vast fortunes from oil, steel, automobiles, and technology, they wound down their careers by giving away their wealth for the betterment of mankind. The foundations created by these business leaders are still providing benefits long after the close of their careers.

The focus of the William and Melinda Gates Foundation is health and education. Grants for health-related programs surpassed $2.5 billion. They include $25 million to the International AIDS Vaccine Initiative and $50 million to the Malaria Vaccine Initiative. One noteworthy grant, a $750 million gift to the Global Fund for Children's Vaccines, creates a global fund in partnership with the World Bank, the World Health Organization, and the Rockefeller Foundation. This fund is intended to support the Global Alliance for Vaccines and Immunization. Closer to home, the Foundation granted more than $100 million to a Seattle-based vaccination program. Bill and Melinda are committed to helping children the world over.

On the education front, the Foundation has committed $1 billion to the United Negro College Fund, for Gates Millennium scholarships to be distributed over 20 years. Libraries have received pledges of $200 million for Internet access. The University of Washington has received $12 million for a law school library that is to be named in honor of Gates's father and $10 million for scholarships in honor of his mother. Additionally, the University of Washington received a $12 million grant for a new biotech building. The Ursuline Academy in Dallas, Texas, where his wife graduated valedictorian, has received $1 million. Finally, Cambridge University has received a pledge of $20 million for a new computing center (Leonard, www.salon.com).

While Bill Gates's philanthropy has helped many organizations, his greatest influence may be with the organization he founded. Microsoft has followed Mr Gates lead and developed its own giving program. In

2001 alone, Microsoft's Giving Program gave over $215 million to help people and communities realize their potential. Since 1983, Microsoft has been following Bill and Melinda Gates's lead by giving back to the communities which have helped make it so exceptionally successful.

Conclusion

History has provided us with many instances of men and women with the vision and ability to create organizations to accomplish great things. This chapter has presented examples of individuals who have had visions of spiritually alive organizations. This vision clearly sees organizations as entities that can be financially success-ful but also use that success for the betterment of society. Each person has addressed the needs of people and society in different ways, but each in his or her own way has created an environment in which all involved can grow. Each has used his or her professional success to build better lives for the employees of the organization and the communities in which it operates.

Chapter 8 in a nutshell

1. In order to address spirituality, an organization must have leadership that is physically and psychologically healthy.

2. An organization itself must be sound financially, to ensure its survival.

3. The leadership of the organization and its members must understand the difference between spirituality and religion.

4. Guided by spiritually vital leadership, a spiritually vital organization can be created.

5. Not only do the members of an organization gain from spirituality in the workplace, so does the entire community.

9

Ethical character

The character that takes command in moments of crucial choices has already been determined by a thousand other choices made earlier in seemingly unimportant moments. It has been determined by all the "little" choices of years past – by all those times when the voice of conscience was at war with the voice of temptation, [which was] whispering the lie that "it really doesn't matter." It has been determined by all the day-to-day decisions made when life seemed far away – the decisions that, piece by piece, bit by bit, developed habits of discipline or of laziness; habits of self-sacrifice or self-indulgence; habits of duty and honor and integrity – or dishonor and shame.

Ronald Reagan, 1993

In a time where few leaders can face the scrutiny of in-depth investigation into their personal lives, the recognition that the profile of a healthy individual includes an examination of character is critical. It is not enough to be physically, psychologically, and spirituality sound. To complete the package, one must examine one's character in order to ensure the optimal use of life. The final piece of the four-dimensional model, our character, can be developed and improved, just as our physical or psychological health can.

> It is not enough to be physically, psychologically, and spirituality sound. To complete the package, one must examine one's character in order to ensure the optimal use of life.

As we have gone through our lives, we have each faced decisions that have become turning points in our lives. These decisions loom large in our memories. They either bring about a sense of pride and contentment for a choice well made or they remind us of our failures; for example, a time when we should have given more consideration to the needs of others or perhaps should have taken a different perspective. What both of these kinds of memories have in common is that they contribute to the person we are. Our character, however, is created and developed by more than just these defining moments of critical choice. Our character is molded and changed each day by the small, seemingly inconsequential decisions we make. It is upon these small choices that we build the strength to face the large decisions that define our lives.

Personal integrity

The definition of character has received much attention in the literature. Some see character as the opposite of personality. Personality is what we show the external world, whereas character is who we really are on the inside. Others see character and personality as virtually interchangeable, with the exception of the morality connotation that character brings to mind. For our purposes, we define ethical character as personal integrity. Integrity is defined as "the state of being unimpaired; soundness or the quality or condition of being whole or undivided; completeness." The individual is undivided in his or her fundamental beliefs and attitudes, presenting those values to everyone.

In *A Better Way To Think About Business*, Robert Solomon (1999) delves into the idea of personal integrity. Solomon describes how integrity is often misunderstood as simply resisting temptation. In reality, someone with personal integrity is often required to take action against an issue that seems unjust or inequitable. The person cannot simply refuse to participate in the behaviors. A person with true integrity must stand up for what he or she believes.

Likewise, people of integrity are often thought of as inflexible and not team players. Refusing to participate in an activity that goes beyond the limits of one's personal values and beliefs does not indicate that the person is not a team player. Rather, this quality, which is perceived as inflexibility, demonstrates a personal level of commitment to ideals that are not open to negotiation. It is a pledge to the wholeness of oneself that is inflexible, not the person.

A perfect example of commitment to one's personal integrity is Admiral Jeremy Michael Boorda (Thomas, Barry, 1996). Admiral Boorda at the age of 56 took his own life on 15 May 1996 in response to news of an investigation into his eligibility to wear the tiny bronze "V" on the medals on his uniform. Many felt that the admiral had every right to wear the medals and could have survived the investigation, but personal integrity was so important to Boorda that he could not face even the mere suggestion of deception on his part.

Admiral Boorda was the first man to ever rise through the ranks of the navy from enlisted man to the navy's top commander. He was well liked, and many referred to him as a "sailor's sailor." He believed in accepting personal responsibility for himself and all who served under him. Shortly before his death, in a speech to the midshipmen of Annapolis, Boorda stated that "every single person in the navy should have one leader they can look to and say, 'that person is responsible and accountable for me.'" Boorda believed that person to be himself.

In true naval tradition, he believed that a captain in battle always goes down with the ship. As the "captain" of the navy, he perceived himself as responsible for everything that went on in the navy whether he was at fault or not. Boorda set himself up as the example to his men and could not tolerate even the slightest questioning of his integrity.

Today, the rules governing the awarding of combat "Vs" are very clear. In 1965, the rules were ambigious and simply stated that "V" pins were authorized for "direct participation in combat operations." Some high-ranking navy officials concluded that he had every right to wear the "V" insignia for valor. Even Arizona Senator John McCain, a former Vietnam prisoner, stated that wearing the decorations "could have been an honest mistake" and that "for someone to allege that he somehow deliberately distorted what was a superb record to me is patently unfair" (Priddy, 1999).

Attempting finally to put the matter to rest for the family of Admiral Boorda and the navy, US Navy Secretary John Dalton signed a memo in which he cited a letter from retired Admiral E. R. Zumwalt, chief of navy operations during Vietnam. In this letter Admiral Zumwalt wrote that Boorda was "clearly authorized" to wear the medals and that wearing them was "appropriate, justified and proper."

Unfortunately in the end, Admiral Boorda did what he felt was right for himself, his family and the navy. A suicide note left by Boorda to the navy or "my sailors," as he called the entire fleet, explained that "he did not wish to be a burden, one more blow to its (the navy's) honor." Boorda chose death rather than living with the challenge to his integrity and that of the navy.

Personality integration

The idea of personality integration is fundamentally relevant to personal integrity. Personality integration is the development of a balanced personality, one having sufficient autonomy, sound principles, and the character to practice these principles in life. In short, it is a wholeness or completeness of the individual.

One aspect of integration that many individuals deal with is the inhibition of emotion. Even for the most integrated of personalities, the tendency to push difficult emotions down and to attempt to forget or ignore them is strong. Research by James Pennebaker on the inhibition of emotions has demonstrated the physical and psychological toll that hiding emotional responses can have. Inhibiting one's emotions can not only adversely affect health issues, but it is also hard work for the inhibitor.

To actively hide one's thoughts, feelings, and behaviors takes physiological work. It can cause immediate biological changes, such as increased heart rate and levels of perspiration. Over time, the effort of inhibiting emotions serves as a cumulative stressor on the body, increasing the probability of illness and other stress-related physical and psychological problems. The more one works at hiding emotions, the greater the stress on the entire system. In addition to health outcomes, ignoring one's emotions also limits the ability to think. By restricting our thinking about a difficult or troublesome event, we fail to engage in broad and integrative thought processes. This process also prevents someone from talking about the event, thereby restricting the understanding and assimilation of the event.

> Over time, the effort of inhibiting emotions serves as a cumulative stressor on the body, increasing the probability of illness and other stress-related physical and psychological problems.

While emotional inhibition is a problem for everyone, it can be an even greater problem for business leaders. As discussed in Chapter 3, managers and executives are often isolated within their organizations. This isolation offers them even less opportunity to talk about emotions or to find outlets to express feelings. An option offered by Pennebaker is writing. By confronting and writing about the difficult emotions we are experiencing, we reduce the effects of the forced inhibition and rethink the facts of the event.

Former president Jimmy Carter is one of the most memorable cases of the physical toll of emotional inhibition. The emotional pressure of four years in office had pronounced aging affects on him. Because of his hands-on management style, it was evident that Carter took personal responsibility for everything that was happening in the country. While he may have had a wonderful and open relationship with his wife Roselyn, this was not sufficient to heal the need for the emotional release he obviously felt. Executives and managers often find themselves in this same isolated position of authority.

Ethical character

Character is not defined simply as an unchangeable aspect of one's personality; rather, it is a more encompassing view that considers one's entire being. Character is the degree to which an individual has the ability to act upon his or her values. It is the strength and conviction to stand your ground and make the morally right decision even when it is difficult. Strength of character means the person has the ability to consider the needs of all involved, not just his or her own needs, and to project those needs into the future, not just to patch together a quick fix for today.

Making decisions regarding an issue that has a clear right answer and a clear wrong answer is easy for anyone. The difficult decisions are the ones in which there is no clear right or wrong answer and in which any decision made will leave someone disappointed, or worse. These situations are where individuals with character make the better decisions. They have the ability to evaluate the situation and make the tough choice when necessary, even when that decision proves to have immediate negative outcomes.

Foundations of character

There are several different ethical foundations upon which a person can develop his or her ethical beliefs. The first is known as *rule-based ethics*, rooted in the work of Immanuel Kant. The work of Kant focuses on the rights and duties of the individual. It states, in broad simplistic terms, that men must lead moral lives and the requirements of morality are always more important than any and all other reasons for doing something when the two contradict each other. Kant required that man must follow the universal imperative that states that man must always be prepared to do whatever moral duty requires regardless of the consequences.

The second foundation is called *consequence-based ethics* and was developed from the writings of well-known philosophers as John S. Mill and Jeremy Bentham. This ethical model directs one's primary focus to the consequences of one's actions. Chosen actions should produce the greatest good for the greatest number and should focus on the end result of actions, not just the obligation to one's duty.

These two ethical frameworks share a common goal in deciding, "what is to be done?" They differ, however, in how to resolve this issue. The consequence-based ethics model purports that "what is good?" must be answered before you can address the question of "what is to be done?" By answering, "what is good?" the individual can then discover the best way to attain the "good." Rule-based ethics states that what is to be done is directed by morality. For example, while a consequence-based ethicist may believe abortion is wrong but in order to save the life of the mother it is acceptable, the Kantian or rule-based ethicist could not accept the termination of the pregnancy even if the life of the mother were lost.

These two ethical models give individuals the foundation for the minimal required actions to which they must adhere. However, they fall short of the third model, *virtue-based ethics*, in offering guidance as to how to be a better person, thereby being a better member of an organization. Recognizing this, many moral philosophers began to return to the Aristotelian view of ethics, which first addresses the individual and then addresses the individual as a member of an organization. In other words, we cannot create ethical organizations by writing policies and procedures. To make an organization ethical, first we must develop ethical employees; then, the organization, as a whole, will naturally follow.

Many people have attempted to define this multifaceted concept of character. In a 1998 sermon, Dr Stephen Murray defined character as "who you are when no one is watching." Kennedy states that one can define his or her character by asking two questions: first, "what is the right thing to do in this situation?" followed by, "What sort of person must I become to be able to do the right thing?" Newman and associates offer that an individual's character is found through answering the question, "who shall I be?" Closely related to Newman's findings is Badaracco's suggestion that we ask ourselves "who am I?" to get at the root of our own character. What all of these definitions have in common is that they describe character as the product of a conscious decision and a commitment to live out the actions of that decision. Aristotle offered a very simple opinion. He saw the person, or rather the character of the person, as the sum of all of his or her previous decisions.

The "good person" and the "good life"

Aristotle was among the first philosophers to directly address the issue of character in the form of virtue-based ethics. In *Nicomachean Ethics*, Aristotle sees virtue-based ethics as the guiding force for defining who we are as people. He stated that we, as individuals, should strive to achieve the "good life" by being the "good person." For Aristotle, the "good life" was achieved by striving to attain the ultimate end. That end for Aristotle was happiness. He felt that happiness was the only thing man desired in and of itself. We don't desire happiness to lead to any other end. We want happiness for its sake alone. All other desires are simply means to other ends. Happiness leads to nothing greater; it is the ultimate end to the good life.

The "good person" for Aristotle was the person who lived the appropriate life to achieve the desired end of happiness. He saw this path as being paved by the virtues. They guided the person in deciding which behaviors would be most beneficial both to the individual's achievement of his or her goals and to the betterment of the community as a whole. By allowing the virtues to set the direction of one's life, Aristotle felt that the person would always have the guidelines by which to evaluate a situation and do the right thing, that which would lead to the "good life."

Aristotle included many character traits under the umbrella of virtues. The many virtues which Aristotle enumerated could be summed into two basic categories. Some virtues were "intellectual," including such elements as wisdom or understanding. These virtues could be taught. They could be demonstrated and cultivated over time. The second category of virtues was "moral," including generosity and self-control. Moral virtues cannot be taught, but rather are formed by habit. They can be observed and imitated. When we see virtuous acts, we learn what virtuous acts are, and, if we choose, we begin incorporating these acts into our lives. We become just by performing just acts, and courageous by performing acts of courage.

An important element of Aristotelian virtue-based ethics is that no trait is ultimately good or bad. Each trait ranges between two extremes. On one end of the continuum is the excess of the trait, and on the other is its deficit. A virtuous person always strives for the appropriate amount of a trait, given the evaluation of a situation. The virtuous choice is somewhere in the middle, one that is neither excessive nor deficient, but the appropriate amount of the trait for the current situation. To be courageous, one must evaluate the situation and display the right amount of courage. Showing too little courage moves one to the deficit, so that the person becomes a coward running from everything. Showing too much courage for the situation moves one to excess, so that the person becomes reckless and needlessly endangered.

> Each time we correctly evaluate a situation and make the right judgment, we strengthen character and move a little closer to being the "good person."

Aristotle's purpose was clear in defining the virtues and their proper use. He wanted others to understand them in order to use them appropriately in striving to achieve the "good life." Each time we correctly evaluate a situation and make the right judgment, we strengthen character and move a little closer to being the "good person." Each new, correct decision strengthens the character we are trying to build.

Others have seen the development of our character in similar veins. Badaracco explains the development of character through the "defining moments" of our lives. As Badaracco explains: "Defining moments challenge us to choose between two or more ideals in which we deeply believe. We form our character in defining moments because we commit to irreversible courses of action that shape our personal and professional." Simmons sees our character development as a process of new decisions. We need to eliminate the decisions that move us away from our ultimate goals and add new decisions that move us in the right direction.

Decision-making

Seeing and understanding that the "good" for me is the same as the "good" for the community is often difficult in the self-centered environment in which many of us live. Once again we are confronted with the dilemma that the apparent solution for the individual and the community may not be the same in the short term, but it is the same when the long term is examined. It is only with the most skillful evaluation of the situation that the person can see that the individual and the community travel the same road to the ultimate end. By building a community of ethical citizens, we ensure an ethical environment for all.

Understanding the relationship between ethical individuals and ethical communities leads us to the next logical step, extending this concept to organizations. Looking at developing ethical organizations from this perspective forces us to re-evaluate how some of the time, effort, and money that companies are spending on ethics officers and programs might be better spent on the ethical development of the employees. By helping individual members of the organization recognize their personal responsibilities to an ethical environment, we may help move the organization well along the path to achieving this goal.

Making the right decisions

A perfect example of seeing the personal need or even the organizational need is the position that The Home Depot took in Florida after Hurricane Andrew. After the destruction left behind by Hurricane Andrew, home-repair companies in southern Florida were charging highly inflated prices for supplies that were needed to make emergency repairs to the homes that remained standing. The devastation was so severe that companies could get almost any price they asked and were taking full advantage of the crisis. The Home Depot made a different choice. They decided to forgo the immediate inflated profits, preferring instead to show their customers and neighbors that they were more interested in helping them than making higher profits. The company decided to address the needs of all, instead of capitalizing on the moment.

The example of The Home Depot demonstrates not only the need to consider the needs of all involved in its decision-making processes, but also the benefits of a long-term perspective as opposed to a short-term one. When the executives of The Home Depot chose integrity instead of profit, they also created a loyalty within their customers that would create more profit over time than the temporarily inflated prices of their competitors would. The company's decision was not only the right thing to do at that moment for the people of south Florida, but it was also the right thing for the company in the long run.

It is often hard to see that certain decisions can be good for everyone. In most cases, any alternative outcome seems to leave a winner and a loser. In many instances, however, this is only the situation when outcomes are considered in the present and a future orientation is ignored.

One situation in which only a long-term perspective was considered was that of the Union Carbide explosion in Bhopal, India (Shrivastava, 1987). CEO Warren Anderson took immediate action when the disaster happened and immediately flew to Bhopal. He took a stand as figurehead for the company, taking personal responsibility for the tragedy. This decision cost him greatly in the few days following the explosion. Anderson was put in jail in India, but was willing to endure the short-term difficulties in order to find a long-term solution that satisfied everyone in the end.

Sometimes it is hard to have the conviction of men like Warren Anderson and hold firm to one's values and beliefs. However, when a person is able to do that, the outcome is better for everyone. Paul Meyer, like Anderson, was willing to stand behind his company and his beliefs. Meyer, CEO of the Success Motivation Institute in Waco, Texas, achieved financial success early in life. By the time he was 27 years of age, Paul was a millionaire from selling insurance, having developed a sales force of over 800 people (Meyer, 1986).

Within a short period of time, Meyer's company had sold so much insurance that Paul was advised by legal counsel that the company did not have enough surplus to cover the amount insured. At the same time it was discovered that his partner was squandering company funds. The lawyer explained that Paul was not directly liable for the problems and that he could simply walk away with his fortune intact. Paul felt, however, that he owed something to the people who had trusted him, so he quickly decided to stay and deal with the crisis. Paul used his personal fortune to pay off the company's creditors. The end result of his decision to stay took two years of Paul's life, cost him his personal wealth, and left him $89,000 in debt. Instead of feeling sorry for himself, however, he believed that he survived with the most important assets he possessed, his integrity, and his good name.

Making the wrong decisions

There are times when making the right decision holds a higher price than one is willing to pay. Other individuals simply want something so badly that they are willing to do anything to obtain the desired outcome. One such example is Joseph P. Kennedy. Kennedy wanted certain things so badly that he was willing to take the easy road rather than risk failure. Kennedy believed that winning was the only thing that was really important. How you won did not matter, as long as you were in the winner's circle when the competition was over. He also clearly conveyed this message to his children. When Kennedy's eldest son, Joe Jr, wanted to letter in baseball at Harvard, Joe Sr bribed the coach to allow his son to be sent into the game long enough to qualify for the letter (Kessler, 1997). There was no concern that the honor meant nothing since it had not been earned. It simply was what he wanted, so his dad bought it for him.

Kennedy demonstrated his lack of concern for making the morally right decision on many occasions. During one of John Kennedy's earliest bids for office, Joseph Kennedy used his money and power to buy votes to ensure that his son would be successful in his political aspirations. Although at the time Joseph Kennedy tampered with the vote there was no evidence that JFK would loose the election, Joseph Kennedy was not going to take the chance of failure.

The lack of character that Joseph Kennedy modeled and eventually passed on to his sons had devastating affects on the family. One of the most devastating was the death of the younger Kennedy. Joe Jr lost his life as a direct result of his learned inability to accept defeat. During a visit home from the war, Joe Jr was present for a large celebration during which brother Jack received a hero's welcome for his role in saving his men when his boat, the PT 109, sank. Taking second place to his brother did not sit well with Joe Jr, and he vowed to return to the war and do something greater than Jack.

Once back in the war, when an opportunity came to fly a very dangerous mission over enemy territory, Joe volunteered. Certain that this mission would gain him greater bravery accolades that Jack, Joe took the mission willingly. He never considered the possibility that he would fail. He had never failed before; Joe Sr had made sure of that. Unfortunately, the senior Kennedy encountered something he could not buy or control. Joe Jr died on that dangerous mission. He died trying to win the attention of his father and the rest of his circle of family and friends at home.

Joseph Kennedy is not alone in his willingness to do anything to win. Unfortunately, the world is full of people like him. Thankfully, however, there are many individuals who are willing to take the more difficult path and make the difficult decisions that will ultimately lead to the best outcome for all. Winston Churchill demonstrated such character during World War II.

At the height of the war, one of the main missions of the allied forces was to break the communication code of the German troops. English spies were successful in doing this and went to Churchill with the decoded message. The translation told a terrible story of a planned bombing of a small town. The military officers wanted to act upon this information immediately. But Churchill decided to remain silent about cracking the code. While he realized that taking action would save the lives of those in the targeted village, Churchill also realized that saving the village meant revealing the fact that agents had successfully broken the code. Revealing this information would save a few hundred lives but would prevent the allies from gaining greater information and, it was hoped, ending the war. Although a difficult decision, Churchill was willing to live with the emotional burden of choosing to let the villagers die in order to save more lives in the long run.

Many philosophers and theologians would consider this a perfect example of "dirty hands." The concept of dirty hands holds that in certain cases a person must dirty their hands a little in order to do something of greater value. In this case, Churchill was willing to sacrifice a few hundred lives in order to end the war and save many thousand lives. It is hard to imagine the emotional and psychological impact a decision such as this may cause an individual. We have all benefitted because Churchill had the strength of character to make such a difficult decision.

Character and the organization

Many organizations express their commitment to ethical character through published mission statements, policies, or credos. Johnson & Johnson is one such company. Johnson & Johnson has made its credo a central focus of the company and a standard by which everyone should live. The credo states in part that the company's first responsibility is to the medical professionals and families who use its products and services. It states that the company must be responsible to its employees and the communities in which it operates. Finally, the credo states that the company must also be responsible to its stockholders and make a fair profit. This credo states in detail the responsibility the company has to all it touches. This credo has been at the foundation of everything that Johnson & Johnson has done since Robert Wood Johnson wrote it in the mid-1940s.

One of the most documented cases of Johnson & Johnson walking the walk of its credo occurred in 1982, when seven people died from cyanide-laced Tylenol. Unlike other companies that delay until the last possible moment to recall a product, Johnson & Johnson immediately recalled all Tylenol from retail shelves. The company also used the media to inform the public about the crisis. Company officials offered to exchange all Tylenol capsules that had already been purchased for Tylenol tablets. It was estimated that, due to the product tampering, Johnson & Johnson suffered a $1.24 billion decline in wealth. This was estimated to be approximately 14 percent of the forecasted value of the company, a decline from which many predicted the company would never recover.

In the early fall of 1982 at the time of the tampering, Tylenol enjoyed 37 percent of the market for over-the-counter painkillers. Stock price and market share fell drastically following the October crisis. By the end of the year, however, Tylenol held a 24 percent share. Tylenol continued to gain market share through the winter and by spring had regained its original position. When asked why Johnson & Johnson was willing to take such a strong position in response to the tampering, company president David R. Clare said: "It was the credo that prompted the decisions that enabled us to make the right early decisions that eventually led to the comeback phase." Lawrence Foster, Vice-President of Johnson & Johnson at the time of the poisonings, explained (1983) what Robert Johnson had outlined for his company some 40 years earlier in the credo – that the company has responsibility to "consumers and medical professionals using its products, employees, the communities where its people work and live, and its stockholders." Johnson believed that if his company stayed true to these responsibilities, his business would flourish in the long run. The credo he wrote was not only moral but profitable as well.

For a company's credo to be more than just words, the company and its leadership must live the credo, not just pay it lip service. Johnson & Johnson proved its credo to be more than rhetoric with the manner in which it handled the Tylenol disaster. The leadership of Johnson & Johnson lived their credo when, without hesitation, they removed Tylenol from the shelf. There was no delay to evaluate the cost of removing the product versus lawsuits for loss of life as the Ford Motor Corporation did with the Pinto automobile (Gioia, 1992). The first and only concern for the management of Johnson & Johnson was the lives of their customers.

Conclusion

As we have seen, personal character goes well beyond the benefit to self. An executive or manager possessing strong character can be an asset to all around him or her. In addition to character touching the lives of those in our immediate personal and professional environments, men and women of character running our organizations will create a better world for everyone.

While character and personal integrity are important for everyone to possess, it is especially important for those individuals who affect the lives of others: the men and women who manage our organizations and become role models for the people who work for them. With people of true integrity running the major corporations, the world can only become a better place in which to live.

Chapter 9 in a nutshell

1. Integrity is having the personal character to behave in a manner consistent with who the person claims to be.

2. Our character develops from taking personal responsibility for our decisions and the actions brought about by those decisions.

3. Decision-making is directed by the ethical foundation in which we believe: does the person follow the rules, evaluate the consequences or make his or her decision based on the determination of the best course of action, given the entire context of the situation?

4. Character increases in strength each time we make a difficult decision and stand by it.

5. The stronger we build our character the easier it is to make the difficult decision.

Part IV

The self-reliant executive

10

A secure platform for achievement and success

True individual freedom cannot exist without economic security and independence. People who are hungry and out of a job are the stuff of which dictatorships are made.

The hopes of the Republic cannot forever tolerate either undeserved poverty or self-serving wealth.

Franklin Delano Roosevelt,
32nd president of the United States (1933–45),
led the nation out of the Great Depression.

The core thesis of this book is that an executive's health is the secure platform for achievement and success. Balanced attention to one's health and well-being is essential to sustained, long-term achievement. Conversely, the failure to attend to one's health places the executive or manager at risk of failure and, in the extreme, of death. An extension of this thesis is that executives and managers should identify their strengths as well as their limitations and vulnerabilities in order to build on the former and guard against the latter. The core of our executive health model is the knowledge and practice of preventive medicine.

> Balanced attention to one's health and well-being is essential to sustained, long-term achievement. Conversely, the failure to attend to one's health places the executive or manager at risk of failure and, in the extreme, of death.

In this concluding chapter we briefly summarize the book, place emphasis on the role of balance in health, present guidelines from our successful and healthy executive profiles, and discuss the importance of self-reliance as the means to building healthy, secure networks. These are challenging and changing times fraught with risks *and* opportunities for executives and managers. Those who lead organizations are called on to be strong, healthy, and secure, in order to help themselves and the organizations they lead to meet the challenges of this new millennium. Those who maintain their physical and psychological health can find success and overcome adversity as they contribute to the greater well-being through vibrant business and economic activity around the world.

A summary of the book

Chapter 1 paints a picture of the stressful and challenging environment faced by executives and managers as a result of globalization, increasing industrial competitiveness, and increasing job insecurity. These processes are placing executives and managers in a vice-grip that saps their strength and sense of security. While these are stressful and challenging times, we argue that businessmen and businesswomen have always faced stressful and challenging times. Business is a risky and challenging profession in which the strong survive.

Chapter 1 also presents an executive health model that considers health-risk factors and strength factors for executives and managers. Most executives and managers understand this point as well as the contemporary forces that contribute to their risks and challenges. But what an executive or manager may overlook is the importance of placing his or her health and self-care high on the priority list of daily tasks and activities. This omission is risky and can lead to serious problems, both for the executives or managers themselves as well as for the organizations and people they lead. Healthy executives can also contribute to the public well-being of the communities in which they work and live. Thus, a good preventive health-management program is an essential tool for the successful executive.

Health-risk factors: threats to executive health

In addition to the many benefits of executive and managerial work, there are also health risks that executives must identify and manage. The four health-risk factors of concern for executives are the Achilles' heel phenomenon, the loneliness of command, work demands and stress, and crisis and failure. These are discussed in the four chapters of Part II in the book.

The Achilles' heel phenomenon refers to the executive's unique inherited and/or acquired health vulnerability. Family medical history is an important source of information about the particular vulnerabilities that an executive may have, such as the risk of cardiovascular disorders, depressive disorders, or other vulnerabilities. These are predisposing health risks but they should not be thought of as predetermining factors. While these health risks may be present, their identification can lead to preventive actions and early interventions to avert their adverse effects. Identifying and then managing health vulnerabilities is a key tenant of preventive medicine.

Loneliness of command is a unique health risk factor for CEOs and other socially isolated senior executives. While leaders, executives, and senior managers may be thought of as strong and solitary figures, they are not beyond the need for reassurance, a sense of felt security, and a secure contact with reality. In fact, executives' dependency needs are normal and healthy aspects of the human condition, even if they can at times cause executives some discomfort. The limitations of finding peers within one's own organization in whom to confide may lead executives and managers to become more isolated than is advisable or healthy.

Work demands, stress, and travel are a third important category of health-risk factor for executives. The average workweek for many executives is 60 to 70 hours, during which there are diverse organizational stakeholders with whom executives must interact. Executives and CEOs are hardly exempt from these pressures and forces on the competitive battlefield. While travel stress created one set of health risks for executives and managers before September 11, 2001, there are different sets of vulnerabilities and health risks occasioned after that date. Finally, performance pressures are among the most important work demands executives must manage.

Business crises and failures may be the most traumatic health-risk factors for executives. These include business disruptions, temporary crises, industrial accidents, bankruptcies, personal threats, or even physical attacks on an executive. In his classic research on healthy, long-term life adjustment, George Vaillant found some trauma or crisis in the experience of each and every person interviewed and studied. The crisis or trauma, however, was not the defining feature of the person's life; rather, the defining feature was how the person managed and coped. Therefore, executives and managers must anticipate crisis and failure at some point in their careers.

Strength factors: enhancing health

While it is important to identify, understand, and manage health-risk factors, they are only one category for executive concern. The second important category for executive concern is the strength factors. A key principle in preventive medicine and in positive psychology is to build strength. The strength factors discussed in the four chapters of Part III in the book are physical fitness, executives' networks of professional and personal relationships, stress-management skills, and balanced investments across several domains of life.

The research and evidence supporting the value of physical fitness for health is well established. Executives can achieve optimal fitness through exercise and diet, with attention to cardiovascular or aerobic fitness, flexibility, and appropriate physical strength. Optimal fitness enhances psychological health as well as physical health. Physical fitness should not be equated with athletic prowess, for an executive or manager need not be athletic to be physically fit. There are various physical fitness activities, such as brisk walking, that do not involve athletics.

> The network of professional and personal relationships that executives build over the years becomes a safety net through which they can construct a fallback position as an alternative course of action if the present situation falls through.

Executives draw strength from rich networks of personal and professional relationships. By drawing on feedback, advice, and moral support from family and friends, Levinson rightly suggests that executives can find strength through relationships to enable them to thrive in this new age of self-reliance. The network of professional and personal relationships that executives build over the years becomes a safety net through which they can construct a fallback position as an alternative course of action if the present situation falls through.

However, relationships cannot substitute for personal stress-management skills, such as planning, time management, relaxation, spiritual disciplines, and cognitive/behavioral skills. Executives and managers must have a set of self-care tools that enable them to be in control and to self-regulate in the most difficult and challenging times. Thus, personal stress-management skills become a complementary form of preventive stress management in difficult and trying times, enhancing the executive's and manager's self-confidence and sense of power.

Finally, seeking balance in life is a great strength factor for executives and managers. The importance of balance in health can be traced back to the great Greek physician Hippocrates, who considered balance within the body a key to health, and imbalance a risk for disease. We suggest that balance in one's life-domain investments is essential to an executive's health. Analogously, just as most financial-investment strategies call for diversity in a portfolio, a health-investment strategy calls equally for diversity in one's life and work investments.

Seeking balance in work and life

The strength found in work–life balance deserves some additional attention in this final chapter because it is so important. The health risks associated with over-attention to work, excessive and obsessive work activities, and preoccupation with work activities can be traced back to 1869 in the clinical observations of Von Deuch. His was the first critical observation of the role overwork can play in cardiovascular problems. Variations on this original observation were subsequently made by William Osler in the early 1900s and then separately by Stewart Wolfe and the cardiology team of Friedman and Rosenman. Certainly inattention to one's work is not desirable and carries with it an entirely different set of risks as well as problems. Therefore, these two extremes are unhealthy ones for an executive or manager to pursue. Preoccupation and obsession with one's work carries risk to personal health and family, while lack of attention to one's work carries the risk of poor performance and the loss of one's job.

How then can an executive or manager strike a balance? That is the challenging work of seeking balance between one's work life and striving for excellence in all that one does. From an Aristotelian perspective, this is to seek happiness by acting in a way that is virtuous but not extreme. This is an effortful activity to optimize one's work and non-work life investments. While it is easy to get angry, it is hard to get angry to the right degree with the right person at the right time. To do so requires the development of self-control and personal skills for acting in a virtuous or good manner. This is the heart of the art and skill of good management. The most dramatic case of the risk of failure to balance one's achieve-

The Balanced Life

Strengths Equal Risks

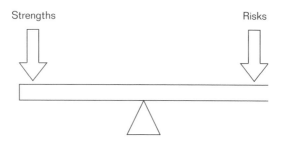

ment drive with self-care and time for rest and relaxation may be that of John D. Rockefeller Sr, who so overworked in the early years that he nearly worked himself to death by his early 50s. The second half of his life reflected the effortful activity of redressing the imbalance, spending more time in other than immediately productive activity, and supporting his son John D. Jr in structuring what became the vast Rockefeller philanthropic trusts.

Guidelines for healthy success and achievement

We have concluded, based upon our biographical research and professional work with executives and managers, that there is no single model or set of rules that can ensure one's health, achievement, and success. There are several successful models that have emerged from the biographical profiles, but one is not necessarily better than the other. Thus, one cannot conclude that all healthy, successful executives get regular physical exercise. One cannot say that each healthy, successful executive meditates or prays on a regular basis. Nor can one say that each successful executive has a religious life in one or another of the world's great religions. While these may be pathways to health and success for some, they may not be the pathways for all.

Thus, what does emerge is the uniqueness of each executive, each manager, and each profile. With this said, executives should not ignore a number of useful guidelines to use for enhancing their health. Rather, they must tailor and individualize these guidelines to fit his or her personal life history, personal preferences, and unique circumstances. In addition, there are two generalizations that do seem to hold as guiding principles for action. First, building on one's strengths and abilities while identifying and then managing one's weaknesses appears central to each of the successful executive profiles we have found. Second, healthy and successful executives are plugged in to professional, personal, and other sustaining relationships with peers, family, faith-based groups, or professional networks. They are not Lone Rangers.

> Building on one's strengths and abilities while identifying and then managing one's weaknesses appears central to each of the successful executive profiles we have found.

The challenging and hard work of executive life does take its toll, and therefore self-care and self-management become central to an executive's well-being. This is no truer than for the chief executive of the United States, the president. One need only look at the average age of the United States presidents to know that they die younger than their contemporaries. The three guidelines, which we explore here, are these:

1. Build strength and develop your natural abilities.
2. Identify and manage your weaknesses and vulnerabilities.
3. Accept and rise above losses and traumas.

Build strength and develop natural abilities

Every executive is endowed with a set of natural abilities and talents. These should become the central foundation for building healthy success and achievement, because they represent the positive essence of the executive's identity. No one can become other than who one is, if one is to live with integrity. There are a number of executives who exemplify this guideline, possibly the most pronounced of these being Theodore Roosevelt, the youngest president in American history. Others include J. P. Morgan Jr, Andrew Carnegie, Bill Gates, and Joseph P. Kennedy.

> Every executive is endowed with a set of natural abilities and talents. These should become the central foundation for building healthy success and achievement, because they represent the positive essence of the executive's identity.

The legacy of Theodore Roosevelt was that of a strong and robust executive who had begun life as a somewhat weak and asthmatic child.

The Life of Strength

Strengths Outweigh the Risks

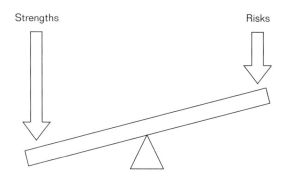

Rather than focusing on his limitations and weaknesses, however, Roosevelt invested time and energy lifting weights and developing the physical gifts he had. He developed his natural abilities and emphasized his strengths, both physically and emotionally. He became a very strong and active adult, famous for his charge up San Juan Hill as the colonel in the Rough Riders. His profile in American history epitomizes the strong and forceful leader acting out of strength and conviction.

John P. Morgan Jr was a leading American executive who very much displayed his own strength, carving a life in contrast to that of his famous father J. P. Morgan Sr. While J. P. Sr lived a very extravagant and flamboyant life, through which he largely ignored his family and focused all his attention on work, John P. Jr crafted an independently successful life that mirrored that of his father rather than modeling it. While the father lived much in the spotlight, he also displayed behaviors that his son vowed never to repeat. The son showed great strength when standing in the shadow of such a strong and famous father. While many sons simply model and replicate the lifestyle and behavior of their fathers, healthy or not, there are those discriminating sons who are able to exercise wise and independent choice. John P. Jr was successful in breaking the cycle of his father's behavior and, while professionally just as successful, led a life that was also committed to family and friends. Though he did show occasional flashes of his father's quick temper, he developed interpersonal skills as one of his greatest strengths.

Andrew Carnegie was known neither for his physical prowess nor for standing tall in the shadow of a famous father. Rather, he was known for his extraordinary philanthropy, which was anchored in his faith and his integrity. These two were the pillars of his strength. He was also known for his treatise "Wealth" in the *North American Review* (1899), which later became known as the gospel (good news) of wealth. For Carnegie, the wealthy were only stewards of the money and financial resources at their disposal, which he thought they must return to the society and community from whence it came. Hence, one of his great strengths was rising above his own needs to address the needs of others. Through the Carnegie Foundation, he built libraries and established support funds to help financially the families of individuals who died or were injured in a heroic act. By the end of his life in 1919, Andrew Carnegie had donated more than $350 million to better the lives of those around him (Wall, 1992).

Microsoft's Bill Gates is the first executive in a century to rival, and then exceed, the philanthropy of Andrew Carnegie. Gates appears to share Carnegie's insight concerning wealth and to also have a philosophy on wealth similar to that of his contemporary, Warren Buffett. As the richest man in the world, Gates has seized the opportunity to give back to the country that helped him earn his fortune, recognizing that historical circumstance as much as personal or collective effort led to his fortune. Gates and his wife, Melinda, have accepted the personal challenge of addressing world health. Though contested by his peers, Gates recently stated that technology was not the answer to all the world's problems. He has focused some of his foundation resources on health care, working in part with the World Health Organization. In this vein, the Gateses have donated over $5.5 billion of their own personal fortune to provide medical help and research for the underprivileged of the world (Hafner, 1999). While no other executive in the world can give at Gates's level, many executives do give generously through alternative vehicles, such as the Rotary Foundation.

One of Joseph P. Kennedy's great strengths was his ability to develop relationships and to network. As with any strength, when taken to the extreme, it becomes a problem. Kennedy was an individual whose unrelenting drive and ambition led him to abuse the influence and power of his strong network of associates. Kennedy had grown up in an environment that approved the unhealthy use of political power. His father, Patrick, had been an influential member of the Boston Irish community and had used his influence over his friends and associates to gain a stronghold in Boston's Ward Eight (Whalen, 1964). These same lessons came from Kennedy's father-in-law, John F. "Honey Fitz" Fitzgerald. The abuse of power was in turn passed on to Joseph Kennedy's sons at an early age. When Joe Jr was concerned about not lettering during his last year at Harvard, Joseph P. intervened, using his "persuasion": he and his friends convinced the coach to allow Joe Jr to play for one inning to ensure his lettering (Kessler, 1997).

Whether through the physical prowess of Teddy Roosevelt or the faith and integrity of Andrew Carnegie, each of these five men stood on their strength in their drive for success and achievement. These strengths contributed to their health and well-being in the midst of their effortful striving.

Identify and manage weaknesses and vulnerabilities

In addition to every executive's endowment of natural abilities and talents, every executive also has weaknesses and vulnerabilities that threaten his or her health and achievement. While the strengths are the foundation for building healthy success and achievement, the weaknesses and vulnerabilities, if not identified and well managed, can erode or undercut even the best foundation. There are a number of executives whose weaknesses and vulnerabilities were identified and well managed, so as neither to unduly damage their health nor hinder their achievements and contributions. We look here at the cases of Winston Churchill, John D. Rockefeller Sr, Michael Eisner, and the unusual case of Robert S. McNamara.

Before we touch on these successful cases, let us first recall the cases of John Curtis Jr and J. Clifford Baxter, both of whom failed to manage their weaknesses and vulnerabilities, which led to tragedy. Each committed suicide, but under very different circumstances. John Curtis Jr appeared to have an ideal life as the new chief executive of Luby's Cafeterias in the mid-1990s. He was married to his high school and college sweetheart, and they had three children. Curtis was active in his church and in civic organizations. He had been with Luby's for 18 years, and was groomed to take over as CEO. The organization was doing well, and nothing seemed as if it should be causing the 49-year-old undue pressure, so it was a surprise when he slit his own throat in a cheap motel after only three months in the job. Clifford Baxter's experience was quite different as a retired senior executive from Enron. At what appeared to be a period of vindication for his expressed concerns about the Houston energy giant's accounting methods, Mr Baxter took his own life in his early 40s. Weakness and vulnerability, however, need not result in suicide and death.

Winston Churchill is an excellent example of one who was aware of his vulnerability to clinical depression and who developed several strategies for the healthy management of this vulnerability. An executive's psychological health is critically important for logical and effective decision-making. While the crafting of sound decisions is critical in any organization, it is nowhere more important than in a nation at war. Such was the case for Winston Churchill, who was prime minister of England during World War II, when the future of the world hung in the balance. Throughout his adult life, Churchill experienced episodes of depression, which he managed through physical activity and rich, emotionally expressive communication, such as letters, with his wife Clementine. Thus, by carefully managing his episodes of depression, Churchill was able to rise above this problem, and led the country to victory during the war. He was so successful in managing this risk that during his time in office few knew of the psychological problems he faced.

John D. Rockefeller Sr's vulnerability was quite different. We have previously shown his weakness and vulnerability to be a distrusting, obsessive, and miserly personality. In many ways during the first half of his life, Rockefeller was like Scrooge. He worried incessantly about losing his wealth and enjoyed none of the fruits of his labor. His personality and behavior were so extreme during that period in his life that he was even estranged from his own brother (Carnegie, 1984). Rockefeller was brought to his senses in his mid-50s, when digestive problems became crippling in such a way that he could hardly eat. Even keeping milk and soda crackers down was a challenge. In addition, he had begun to lose all of his hair. The doctors had little hope of his survival if he did not change. He was literally killing himself. At this point Rockefeller made a decision to stop worrying about losing his money, determining instead to enjoy it himself and to share his wealth with others. By managing this personality weakness and vulnerability, he renewed his life. He overcame

The Life at Risk

Risks Outweigh Strength

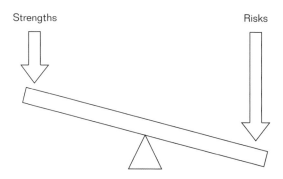

his fears and found comfort and true joy in sharing what he had gained. Instead of dying alone at 53, Rockefeller lived constructively to 98 and used his wealth to improve the lives of millions around the world.

Michael Eisner's vulnerability was not psychological, but rather it was cardiovascular. In July 1994, Eisner underwent quadruple-bypass surgery to enhance his cardiovascular health and prevent a heart attack. Heart disease is not a sudden problem, as we saw earlier in the book; rather, it is a chronic, long-term health problem, the leading cause of death in the industrialized nations. Eisner was also central to The Disney Company's health, given his leadership alongside the late Frank Wells in restoring Disney's image and profitability in the ten years beginning in 1984. While Disney's stock price dropped with the announcement of his surgery, Eisner had a quick recovery, and within two days of his return, the stock price rose by $5 per share, and continued to rise (Huey, 1995). This was much better for the company than when the legendary Walt Disney had cancer in 1967. When Wall Street heard of Disney's death, the company's stock dropped substantially (Worrell *et al.*, 1986). Fifteen years later, the *Wall Street Journal* still questioned whether the company had recovered.

Robert S. McNamara's case is unusual in that he gave the impression of having not the least weakness nor vulnerability. He is actually an excellent example of apparently effective coping, coupled with cross-over stress effects. When an executive gives the appearance of the effective management of stress or crisis, only to transfer the burden of adjustment to his or her spouse, then cross-over effects can be seen (Westman, Etzion, 1995). During the Vietnam conflict, when the decisions of McNamara were sending thousands of young men to their deaths, he seemed to cope with the stress extremely well. Many marveled at his ability to remove himself from the emotional side of the work he was doing. Some felt he went too far in removing himself and that he had become completely dispassionate about the number of lives his decisions were costing the country (Byrne, 1993). What many at the time did not know, however, was that McNamara's wife was suffering from severe stomach ulcers brought on by her husband's job.

Weakness and vulnerability are human characteristics that executives must identify and manage within themselves to prevent their adverse effects. These vulnerabilities include both psychological risks, such as clinical depression in the case of Winston Churchill, and physical disorders, such as cardiovascular disease in the case of Michael Eisner. These men managed their problems well. So too did Robert McNamara, but his wife was the one to pay the price for the burden McNamara bore.

Accept and rise above losses and traumas

Loss and trauma are experiences that all executives have experienced and can expect. In his landmark Grant Study report, George Vaillant found that every subject in his 35-year study period had experienced some trauma or loss. However, it was neither the trauma nor the loss that characterized the life. Rather, healthy members of the study accepted these difficult experiences and rose above them in moving on with their lives. This core lesson is also reflected in the life experiences of a number of leading executives, such as Franklin D. Roosevelt, Katherine Graham, Sir John Templeton, and Lee Iacocca.

Franklin D. Roosevelt was best known for his leadership of the United States through the Great Depression and World War II, some of the most difficult times for the nation in the twentieth century. Although Roosevelt was an active politician, a reassuring speaker during his fireside chats, and a powerful world leader, he was also crippled by polio during his most productive years. How could this be? Roosevelt was not born with polio, but rather contracted the disease in young adulthood. This disease led to the loss of the use of his legs, leaving him with a lifelong disability. Comparatively few people knew of Roosevelt's disability during his years of national leadership, because of his extensive efforts to conceal it. He built his upper body strength to enable him to partially compensate for his loss, and he relied on others' help, lending him their legs and their strength. Roosevelt accepted his personal loss and then rose above it with a variety of effortful activities and strategies.

Katharine Graham is another example of an executive who overcame personal loss and tragedy, rising to a challenging occasion. The sudden and unexpected death of her bright but mercurial husband Phil Graham left Katharine with one of the largest and arguably most respected newspapers in the country. Although *The Washington Post* was originally owned by Katharine's father, Phil Graham had managed the paper since their marriage, while Katharine had remained home raising the couple's children. By the time of her husband's suicide, Katharine had forgotten any idea of a career in journalism. She had become the wife of a successful man and spent her time in the role of wife and mother. With his death, Katharine had either to lose the *Post*, which had been in the family for years, or to find the courage to face her fears and to master the challenge of executive leadership. She did find that courage and was able to develop a strong, diverse network of friends and colleagues through which she found strength as well as knowledge. Katharine Graham became one of the most successful and respected journalists of the twentieth century.

Sir John Templeton was another executive who experienced the tragic loss of his wife of many years. In Templeton's case, however, instead of throwing him out of balance, this tragedy helped him to recognize the need for balance in his life. Sir Templeton realized after the death of his wife that even though we may get things wrong in the first part of our lives, we have an opportunity to correct them (Berryessa, Kurzner, 1988). After spending the first half of his life working long, hard days on Wall Street, Templeton, like John D. Rockefeller, decided that there was something missing in his life. In 1987, Templeton established the John Templeton Foundation, which utilizes his personal funds to support over 100 programs worldwide. The foundation, through his personal guidance, has added significantly to the monetary value of the Nobel Prizes and other programs that promote the foundation's primary goals. These goals include stimulating serious links between science and all religions, promoting an appreciation of character-building, and encouraging an appreciation of the benefits of freedom. A personal touch in Templeton's movement beyond the loss of his wife came from his son. Recognizing his father's loss, grief, and need, Templeton's son began to orchestrate a relationship between his father and a widowed neighbor. The relationship blossomed into Templeton's second marriage.

Lee Iacocca was not quite as fortunate. He too lost his wife and partner in what would become a personal crisis for him. The crisis faced by Lee Iacocca was the death of Mary, his wife of 37 years. After her death, Iacocca's life got out of balance, and he seemed to begin a search to replace the void left by Mary's death. In the next 11 years, he married and divorced twice. Both marriages were to younger women, and neither lasted for more than three years. While neither marriage succeeded in rebuilding the balance, he seems to have found his stability on his own.

Loss and trauma can break some executives, just as unmanaged weaknesses and vulnerabilities can lead to tragedy. However, they need not. Executives who accept the loss and rise above the trauma are able to move on, living healthy lives and having productive careers.

Self-reliance and secure networks

Self-reliance is a paradoxical term referring to the interdependence of an executive who recognizes his or her natural dependency needs and realistically accepts responsibility for them. The common connotation of self-reliance as independence is a fantasy and myth which executives best overcome for their own long-term health and well-being. Self-reliance, as we understand the term, embodies an acceptance of strengths, weaknesses, and vulnerabilities. Rather

> The common connotation of self-reliance as independence is a fantasy and myth which executives best overcome for their own long-term health and well-being.

than pursue the fantasy expressed in Harold Geneen's "If I had enough arms and legs and time, I'd do it all myself," self-reliant executives reach out to others at their points of limitation and draw on the strengths and talents of those with whom they work. This process of building healthy attachments leads to secure networks, even safety nets, for the difficult and challenging times which business offers every executive and manager some time in their career. Hence, developing self-reliance and secure networks are among the strong, preventive health-management medicines for the successful executive.

Chapter 10 in a nutshell

1. Build strength and develop your natural abilities.

2. Identify and manage your weaknesses and vulnerabilities.

3. Accept and rise above losses and traumas.

4. Executive health is the cornerstone of a good life, not the end product.

5. Take responsibility for your gifts and assets, sharing generously and receiving graciously.

Appendix
Health assessments
and referrals

Despite the best-laid plans in business and life, problems and unexpected events arise. The healthy executive is in the best position to address problems and the unexpected. As a means of developing good information about health and health habits, executives may use one or both of two different self-administered diagnostic instruments. These instruments are the Stress & Coping Inventory (SCI) and ASSET. In addition, executives should feel free to use professional experts with regard to their own health. While there is much an executive can do in terms of self-care and health enhancement, there are professionals who stand ready to further support an executive in health enhancement and disorder prevention. These professionals include physicians, psychologists and psychiatrists, clergy and chaplains, philosophers and ethicists, and should be treated as members of the executive's personal staff. These professionals help extend the strength and ability of high-performance executives.

Centers of excellence in executive health generally fall into two broad categories: preventive-medicine orientation; and mental-health orientation. The former is much more common. Leaders in preventive medicine are the Cooper Clinic in Dallas, Texas; the Duke Executive Health Program in Durham, North Carolina; the John Hopkins Executive Health Program in Baltimore, Maryland; the Mayo Clinic Executive Health Program in Rochester, Minnesota; and the Cleveland Clinic Executive Health Program in Cleveland, Ohio. The Menninger Clinic in Topeka, Kansas, has been a leader in executive mental health.

Some executives may prefer to develop some self-assessment information prior to drawing on professional or clinic-based diagnostic services.

The Stress & Coping Inventory is available from Richard H. Rahe, MD, Health Assessment Programs, Inc., 638 St. Lawrence Ave, Reno, NV, 89509, USA, 702/348-8586, www.DrRichardRahe.com. The SCI provides an executive with detailed information in three broad categories:

- health history, risks, stress and strain
    - biological and biographical endowment
    - recent life changes
    - recent physical and psychological health
    - health-risk behaviors and emotions
- healthy habits and coping resources
    - healthy habits, diet, and exercise
    - problem-solving abilities
    - social supports from family and friends
    - life satisfactions from faith and humor
- life balance

ASSET is available from RCL Ltd, Williams House, Manchester Science Park, Lloyd Street North, Manchester, M15 6SE, UK (fax 44 161 870 3333 591) www.robertsoncooper.com. ASSET provides detailed information with a more occupational and organizational orientation:

- sources of job stress and pressure:
    - work relationships
    - work/life balance
    - overload
    - job security
    - control
    - resources and communication
    - pay and benefits
- overall job satisfaction
- attitudes toward your organization
    - organization's commitment to employees
    - employee's commitment to the organization
- health effects of stress and pressure

– psychological well being

– physical health.

Identifying early-warning signs of health problems is one the keys to the prevention of serious health disorders. Some early-warning signs should be used as feedback for some rest and recovery, such as fatigue, lack of energy, and mild discomforts. However, persisting signs such as a depressed mood or sadness, changes in appetite, weight, or sleep habits, generalized anxiety or panic attacks, chest pains, and other physical symptoms should not be ignored.

An executive might follow the same three general guidelines that a general practitioner might follow in the diagnostic process.

1. Be attentive to symptoms and complaints that do not have a known, specific, physical basis, such as chest pains in the absence of organic cardiovascular disease and anxiety or depression without a major life change or trauma.

2. Be attentive to complaints or symptoms that are an over-reaction or prolonged reaction to demands or traumatic life events.

3. Health assessments can be complicated by the compounding of stress-related disorders with more basic psychological disorders, and a knowledgeable mental health professional is required in such cases.

Bibliography

Adair, J. *Effective Time Management*. London: Pan Books, 1982.

Adler, N. E., W. T. Boyce, M. A. Chesney, S. Folkman, and S. L. Syme. "Socioeconomic inequalities in health: No easy solution." *Journal of the American Medical Association*, 269 (1993):3140–45.

Albrecht, K. *Stress and the Manager*. New Jersey: Prentice-Hall, 1979.

American College of Sports Medicines. *Guidelines for Exercise Testing and Prescription*. 4th edn, Philadelphia: Lea and Febiger, 1991.

Aristotle. *The Nicomachean Ethics*. Oxford: Oxford University Press, 1998.

Arthur, H. M., P. E Garfinkel and J. Irvine, "Development and testing of a new hostility scale." *Canadian Journal of Cardiology,* May 15 (5) (1999):539–44,

Astrup, A. "Healthy lifestyles in Europe: prevention of obesity and type II diabetes by diet and physical activity." *Public Health Nutr* '2001, Apr 4' (2B):499–515.

Austin American-Statesman. "Luby's CEO suicide shocks workers' family." March 20 (1997): C1.

Badaracco, J. K. Jr "The discipline of building character." *Harvard Business Review*, 76 (1998): 114–24.

Bahnson, C. B. "Stress and cancer: The state of the art, part 2." *Psychosomatics*, 22 (1981): 207–20.

Baier, K. "Deontelogical theories." *Encyclopedia of Bioethics*. Vol. 1. New York: Free Press, 1978.

Barry, J. "Doing good by eating chicken: A profile of Chick-fil-A Inc.'s Truett Cathy." *Philanthropy,* September/October 1998.

Benson, H. *The Relaxation Response*. New York: William Morrow, 1975.

Benson, H. and M. Stark, *Timeless Healing: The Power and Biology of Belief*. New York: Scribner, 1996.

Bentham, J. *An Introduction to the Principles of Morals and Legislation*. New York: Hafner, 1948.

Berger, B. G., E. Friedman and M. Eaton. "Comparison of jogging, the relaxation response and group interaction for stress reduction". *Journal of Sport and Exercise Psychology*, 10 (1988):431–47.

Berryessa, N. and E. Kirzner. *Global Investing: The Templeton Way*. Hamewood, IL: Dow Jones-Irwin, 1988.

Beschloss, M. R. *Kennedy and Roosevelt: The Uneasy Alliance*. New York: W. W. Norton, 1980.

Bortner, R.W. "A short rating scale as a potential measure of Pattern A behavior". *Journal of Chronic Diseases*, 22 (1969):87–91.

Brenner, J. G. *The Emperors of Chocolate*. New York: Random House, 1999.

Breslow, L. and P. Buell. "Mortality from coronary heart disease and physical activity of work in California". *Journal of Chronic Diseases*, 11 (1960):615–25.

Brinker, N. *On the Brink: The Life and Leadership of Norman Brinker*. Arlington, Texas: Summit, 1996.

British Heart Foundation Health Promotion Research Group. European Cardiovascular Disease Statistics, 2000 edn. Oxford: British Heart Foundation, 2000 (http://www.bhf.org.uk/, accessed 3 March 2002).

British Heart Foundation. British Heart Foundation Statistics Database 2002. Oxford: British Heart Foundation, 2002 (http://www.bhf.org.uk/, accessed 3 March 2002).

Burke, R. J. and E. R. Greenglass. "Work and family." *International Review of Industrial and Organizational Psychology*, 1987.

Byrne, D. G. Invited review. "Personality, life events and cardiovascular disease." *Journal of Psychosomatic Research*, 21 (1987): 666–71.

Byrne, J. A. *The Whiz Kids: The Founding Fathers of American Business and the Legacy They Left Us*. New York: Currency Book, 1993.

Cannon, W. B. *Alternative Satisfactions for the Fighting Emotions. Bodily Changes in Pain, Hunger, Fear and Rage: An Account of Recent Researches into the Function of Emotional Excitement*, New York: Appleton, 1929 (Original work published 1915), 377–92.

Cannon-Bowers, J. A. and E. Salas. *Making Decisions under Stress: Implications for Individual and Team Training*. Washington, DC: American Psychological Association, 1998.

Carlson, C. R., F. L. Collins, A.J. Nitz and E. T. Sturgis. "Muscle stretching as an alternative relaxation training procedure." *Journal of Behavior Therapy and Experimental Psychiatry*, 21 (1990):29–38.

Carnegie, A. "Wealth." *North American Review*, 148 (889): 653–64.

Carnegie, D. *How to Stop Worrying and Start Living*. New York: Pocket Books, 1984.

Carrington, P., G. Collings and H. Benson, "The use of meditation – relaxation for the management of stress in a working population." *Journal of Occupational Medicine*, 22 (1980), 221–31.

Cartwright, S., C.L. Cooper and A. Barron. "Manager stress and road accidents." *Journal of General Management*, 19 (1993):78–85.

Cartwright, S. and C. L. Cooper. *Managing Workplace Stress*. Sage Publications 1998.

Cascio, W. F., C. E. Young, and J. R. Morri. "Financial consequences of employment change decisions in major US corporations." *Academy of Management Journal*, 40 (1997):1175–80.

Cascio, W. F. "Learning from outcomes: financial experiences of 300 firms that have downsized." In M. Gowing, J. Kraft, and J. C. Quick, eds. *The New Organizational Reality*. Washington, DC: American Psychological Association. 1998, 55–70.

Cash, K. C. and G. R. Gray. "A framework for accommodating religion and spirituality in the workplace." *Academy of Management Executive,* 14 (2000):124–34.

Chernow, R. *Titan: The Life of John D. Rockefeller Sr.* New York: Random House, 1998.

Churchill, W. S. *Painting as a Pastime*. Introduction by Os Guinness. Virginia: The Trinity Forum, 2001 (Original essay published in London by Odhams Press Ltd, 1948.).

Cook, W. W., and D. M. Medley. "Proposed hostility and pharisaic-virtue scales for the MMPI." *Journal of Applied Psychology*, 38 (1954):414–18.

Cooper, C. L. *Handbook of Stress, Medicine, and Health*. Boca Raton, FL: CRC, 1996.

Cooper, C. L. and S. Cartwright. "Healthy mind, healthy organization: A proactive approach to occupational stress." *Human Relations*, 47 (1994): 455–71.

Cooper, C. L., R.D. Cooper and L. D. Eaker. *Living With Stress*. London: Penguin, 1988.

Cooper, C. L. and M. Kelly. "Stress among blue-collar workers." *Employee Relations*, 3 (1981): 2.

Cooper, C. L. and S. Lewis. *Balancing your Career, Family and Life*. London: Kogan Page, 1997.

Cooper, C. L. and J. C. Quick. *FAST FACTS: Stress and Strain* (clinical monograph). Oxford, England: Health Press, 1999.

Cooper, C. L. and J. Roden. "Mental health and satisfaction among tax officers." *Social Science and Medicine*, 21 (1985):747–51.

Cowley, G. "Bill's biggest bet yet." *Newsweek*, February 4, 2002, 44–49.

Cox, T. *Stress*. Macmillan, London, 1985.

Dattore, P. F. Shontz, and L. Coyne. "Premorbid personality differentiation of cancer and non-cancer groups." *Journal of Consulting and Clinical Psychology*, 48 (1980):388–94.

Davis, M., Eshelman, E. R., and M. McKay. *The Relaxation and Stress Reduction Workbook* (4th edn) Oakland, CA: New Harbinger, 1995.

DeFrank, R. S., R. Konopaske and J. M. Ivancevich. "Executive travel stress: perils of the Road Warrior." *Academy of Management Executive* 14 (2000):58–71.

de Geus, E. J., Van Doornen, L. J. and J. F. Orlebeke. "Regular exercise and aerobic fitness in relation to psychological make-up and physiological stress reactivity." *Psychosomatic Medicine*, 55 (1993):347–63.

Dembroski, T. M., and J. M. MacDougall. "Behavioral and psycho-physiological perspectives on coronary-prone behavior." In T. M. Dembroski, T. H. Schmidt, and G. Blumchen (eds), *Biobehavioral bases of coronary heart disease*. New York: Karger, 1983, 106–29.

Follett, K. *On Wings of Eagles*. New York: Penguin Books, 1983.

Forbes, J. D. *J. P. Morgan Jr, 1867–1943*. Charlottesville: University Press of Virginia, 1981.

Foster, L. "The Johnson & Johnson credo and the Tylenol crisis." *New Jersey Bell Journal*, 6 (1983):1.

France, M. and M. Arndt. "After the shooting stops." *Business Week* (March 12, 2001): 98.

Freud, S. *The Problem of Anxiety*. New York: The Psychoanalytic Quarterly Press, 1936.

Friedman, M. and R. H. Rosenman. *Type A: Your Behavior and Your Heart*. Knopf, New York, 1974, 266–68.

Friedman M., C. E. Thorensen, and J. J. Gill, *et al.* "Alteration of Type A Behavior and Reduction in Cardiac Recurrences in Post-Myocardial Infarction Patients." *American Heart Journal*, 108 (1984): 237–48.

Frost, P. and S. Robinson. "The toxic handler: organizational hero – and casualty." *Harvard Business Review*, 77 (1999):97–106.

Geletkanyca, M. A. and D. C. Hambrick. "The external ties of top executives: implications for strategic choice and performance." *Administrative Science Quarterly*, 42:654–81.

Gilbert, R. E., *The Mortal Presidency: Illness and Anguish in the White House*. New York: Fordham University Press, 1998.

Gilbert, R. E., ed. *Managing Crisis: Presidential Disability and the Twenty-Fifth Amendment*. New York: Fordham University Press, 2000.

Gioia, D. A. "Pinto fires and personal ethics: A script analysis of missed opportunities." *Journal of Business Ethics*, 11 (1992):379–89.

Gordon, G. "Tending the spirit while watching the bottom line." *New Hampshire Magazine*. August, 2000.

Graham, K. *Personal History*. New York: Alfred A. Knopf, 1997.

Grant, J. M. *The Great Texas Banking Crash: An Insider's Account*. Austin: University of Texas Press, 1996.

Griffin, R. W., A. M. O'Leary-Kelly, and J. Collins, eds. *Dysfunctional Behavior in Organizations: Violent and Deviant Behavior*. Monographs in Organizational Behavior and Industrial Relations, Vol. 23, Parts A and B. Stamford: JAI, 1998.

Groppel, J. L. and B. Andelman. *The Corporate Athlete: How to Achieve Maximal Performance in Business and Life*. New York: John Wiley & Sons, 2000.

Guest, D. and R. Williams. "How home affects work". *New Society*, 23 (1973):114–17.

Guiness, Os, ed. *When No One Sees – The Importance of Character in an Age of Image*. Colorado Springs: Navpress, 2000.

Hacker, L. M. *The World of Andrew Carnegie: 1865–1901*. New York: J. B. Lippincott, 1968.

Hafner, K. "Bill Gates, Wife Donate $3.3 billion." *The Oregonian*, February, 7, 1999 B11.

Hall, B. H. and R. Rhodes. *Living in a Troubled World*. Kansas City, MO: Hallmark Cards. 1981.

Hallowell, E. M. *Connect*. New York: Pantheon Books. 1999.

Hambrick, D. C. "The top management team: key to strategic success." *California Management Review*, 30 (1987):88–108.

Harris, G. T. "Sir John Templeton: mixing science, religion, and humility." *Spirituality & Health*, Fall (2001):36–39.

Hawke, D. F. *John D.: The Founding Father of the Rockefellers*. New York: Harper & Row, 1980.

Hemingway, H., and M. Marmot. "Psychosocial factors in the aetiology and prognosis of coronary heart disease: systematic review of prospective cohort studies." *British Medical Journal*, 318 (1999): 1460–67.

Herrick, T. "Suicide of Luby's CEO attributed to job stress." *Houston Chronicle*, March 15, 1997, 29.

Higgins, J. V. "Outsiders reminded of family clout: past is replete with casualties who crossed the fords." *The Detroit News*, July 27, 2001.

Hinkle, L. E. and S. Wolf. "The effects of stressful life situations on the concentration of blood glucose in diabetic and non-diabetic humans." *Diabetes*, 1 (1952):383.

House, J. S., K. R. Landis, and D. Umberson. "Social relationships and health." *Science* 241 (1988):540–45.

Huey, J. "Eisner explains everything." *Fortune*, April 17, 1995, p. 44.

Hugdahl, K. *Psychophysiology: The Mind–Body Perspective*. Cambridge: Harvard University Press, 2001.

Huyser, General R. E. *Mission to Tehran*. New York: Harper & Row, 1986.

Iacocca, L. *Iacocca: An Autobiography*. New York: Bantam Books, 1984.

Iacocca, L. *Talking Straight*. New York: Bantam Books, 1988.

Jin, P. "Efficacy of Tai Chi, brisk walking, meditation and reading in reducing mental and emotional stress. *Journal of Psychosomatic Research*, 36 (1992):361–70.

Kahn, R. L., D. M. Wolfe, R. P. Quinn, J. D. Snoek and R. A. Rosenthal. *Organizational Stress: Studies in Role Conflict and Ambiguity*. New York: Wiley. 1964.

Kant, I. *Groundwork of the Metaphysics of Morals*. Trans. by H. J. Paton. New York: Harper & Row, 1964.

Kennedy, R. G. "Virtue and corporate culture: the ethical formation of baby wolverines." *Review of Business* 17 (1995–96):10–15.

Kent, H. personal communication, December 30, 1998.

Kessler, R. *The Sins of the Father: Joseph P. Kennedy and the Dynasty he Founded*. New York: Warner Books, Inc., 1997.

Kets de Vries, M. F. R. "Leaders who self-destruct: the causes and cures." *Organizational Dynamics*, 17 (1989):5–17.

Kets de Vries, M. F. R. *Life and Death in the Executive Fast Lane*. San Francisco: Jossey-Bass. 1995.

Kets de Vries, M. F. R., M. Loper and J. Doyle. "The leadership mystique: executive commentary." *Academy of Management Executive*, 8 (1994):73–92.

Kets de Vries, M. F. R., and D. Miller. *The Neurotic Organization*. Jossey-Bass: San Francisco, 1985.

Kilburg, R. R. *Executive Coaching: Developing Managerial Wisdom in a World of Chaos*. Washington, DC: American Psychological Association, 2000.

Killinger, B. *Workaholics: The Respectable Addicts*. Buffalo, NY: Firefly Books, 1991.

Kline, J. Jr, and L. Sussman. "An executive guide to workplace depression." *Academy of Management Executive*, 14 (2000):103–14.

Koskoff, D. E. *Joseph P. Kennedy: A Life and Times*. Englewood Cliffs, NJ: Prentice-Hall, 1974.

D., Kromhout, A. Menotti, H. Kesteloot and S. Sans. "Prevention of coronary heart disease by diet and lifestyle: evidence from prospective cross-cultural, cohort, and intervention studies. *Circulation*, 105 (2002):893–98.

Kubitz, K. A., and D. M. Landers. "The effects of aerobic training on cardiovascular responses to mental stress: an examination of underlying mechanisms." *Journal of Sport & Exercise Psychology*, 15 (1993):326–37.

Kupperman, J. *Character*. New York: Oxford University Press, 1991.

Laird, D. A. *Psychology and Profits*. New York: B. C. Forbes, 1929.

Latham, E., ed. *John D. Rockefeller – Robber Baron or Industrial Statesman?* Boston: D.C. Heath, 1949.

Lazear, J. *The Man who Mistook his Job for a Life*. New York: Crown Publishers, 2001.

Leonard, A. "Is Bill Gates a closet Liberal?" www.salon.com.

Leupker, R. V. "Heart disease." In R. B. Wallace, ed. *Public Health and Preventive Medicine*. Stamford, CN: Appleton & Lange, 1998.

Levinson, H. *The Exceptional Executive: A Psychological Conception*. Cambridge: Harvard University Press, 1968.

Levinson, H. "The abrasive personality." *Harvard Business Review*, 56 (1978):86–94.

Levinson, H. "When executives burn out." *Harvard Business Review*, 59 (1981):73–81.

Levinson, H. and J. C. Wofford. "Approaching retirement as the flexibility phase." *Academy of Management Executive*, 14 (2000):84–95.

Lewis, C. S. *Mere Christianity*. New York: Macmillan, 1979.

Loehr, J. and T. Schwartz. "The making of a corporate athlete." *Harvard Business Review,* 79 (2001): 120–28.

Lowenstein, R. *Buffett: The Making of an American Capitalist*. New York: Random House, 1995.

Lynch, J. J. *A Cry Unheard: New Insights into the Medical Consequences of Loneliness*. Baltimore, MD: Bancroft, 2000.

Mack, D. A. and J. C. Quick, "EDS an inside view of a corporate life cycle transition." *Organizational Dynamics*, 31 (2002):282–93.

Makin, P., C. L. Cooper and C. Cox. *Managing people at work*. London: Routledge, 1988.

Marshall, J. and C. L. Cooper. *Executives Under Pressure*. London: Macmillan, 1979.

Matteson, M. T. and J.M. Ivancevich. "Individual stress management interventions: Evaluation of Techniques." *Journal of Managerial Psychology*, 2 (1987), 24–30.

McCullough, D. *John Adams*. New York: Simon & Schuster, 2001.

McMurray, R. G., P. L. Kocher and S. M. Horvath. "Aerobic power and body size affects the exercise-induced stress hormone response to varying water temperature." *Aviation Space and Environmental Medicine*, 65 (1994): 809–14.

McNamara R. S. and B. Vandemark. *In Retrospect: The Tragedy and Lessons of Vietnam*. New York: David Mckay, 1996.

Mendes de Lwon, C.F., and M. G. Meesters. In A. Appels, J. Groen, J. Koolhaas, J. van Dixhoorn, L. van Doornen, C. Mendes de Leon, and C. Meesters (eds), *Behavioral Observations in Cardiovascular Research*. Amsterdam: Swets & Zeitlinger B.V., 1991, 107–28.

Mettlin, C. "Occupational careers and the prevention of coronary-prone behavior." *Social Science and Medicine*, 10 (1976):367–72.

Meyer, P. J. *The Story of Paul J. Meyer: The Million Dollar Personal Success Plan*. Hollywood, FL: Frederick Fell Publishers, Inc. 1986.

Mill, J. S. *Utilitarianism, Liberty, and Representative Government*. London: Dent, 1910.

Miller, J. D. "The NIOSH-suggested list of the ten leading work-related diseases and injuries. *Journal of Occupational Medicine*, 26 (1984) 340–41.

Miller, T. Q., T. W. Smith, C. W. Turner, M. L. Guijarro and A. J. Hallet. "A meta-analytic review of research on hostility and physical health." *Psychological Bulletin*, 119(2) (1996), 322–48.

Mitroff, I. I. and E. A. Denton. *A Spiritual Audit of Corporate America: A Hard Look at Spirituality, Religion, and Values in the Workplace*. San Francisco: Jossey-Bass, 1999.

Morris, B. "The wealth builders." *Fortune*, December 11:80, 1995.

Morris, B. and N. A. Tarpley. "So you're a player. Do you need a coach?" *Fortune*, 141 (2000):144–50.

Morris, M. *Theodore Rex*. New York: Random House, 2001.

Morris, J. R., W. F. Cascio and C. E. Young. "Downsizing after all these years." *Organizational Dynamics*, Winter, (1999):78–87.

Murphy, P. E. "Character and virtue ethics in international marketing: an agenda for managers, researchers, and educators." *Journal of Business Ethics*, 18 (1999):107–24.

Murray, C. J. L. and A. D. Lopez. "Global and regional cause-of-death patterns in 1990." In C. J. L. Murray and A. D. Lopez, eds. *Global Comparative Assessments in the Health Sector*. Geneva: World Health Organization, 1994.

Murray, S. A. "What is character?" Sermon given at First Presbyterian Church in Arlington, Texas on December 13, 1998.

Neck, C. P. and K. H. Cooper. "The fit executive: exercise and diet guidelines for enhancing performance." *Academy of Management Executive*, 14 (2000):72–83.

Nelson, D. L. and R. J. Burke. "Women executives: health, stress, and success." *Academy of Management Executive*, 14 (2000):107–21.

Newman, J. L., E. A. Gray, , and D. R. Fuqua. "Beyond ethical decision-making." *Consulting Psychology*, 48 (1996):230–36.

Norris, R., D. Carroll and R. Cochrane. "The effects of aerobic and anaerobic training on fitness, blood pressure and psychological stress and well-being." *Journal of Psychosomatic Research*, 34 (1990):367–75.

Ornish, D. *Dr Dean Ornish's Program for Reversing Heart Disease*. New York: Ivy Books, 1990.

Pedersen, D. "A lonely death in Texas" (suicide of Luby's CEO, John E. Curtis Jr). *Newsweek*, March 31, 53 (1997) .

Pennebaker, J. W., ed. *Emotion, Disclosure, & Health*. Washington, DC: American Psychological Association, 1995.

Pennebaker, J.W., ed., *Opening Up: The Healing Power of Expressing Emotions*. New York: Jilford, 1997.

Pincherle, A. "Fitness for work." *Proceedings of the Royal Society of Medicine*, 65 (1972):321–24.

Porter, G. "Organizational impact of workaholism: suggestions for researching the negative outcomes of excessive work." *Journal of Occupational Health Psychology*, 1(1) (1996):70–84.

Powell, H. E., P. D. Thomson, C. J. Caspersen, *et al*. "Physical activity and incidence of coronary heart disease." *Annual Review of Public Health*, 8 (1987):253–87.

Priddy, R. C. "The human whole." http://home.no.net/rrpiddy/psy/, 1999.

Pronk, S. J., N. P. Pronk, A. Sisco and D. S. Ingalls. "Impact of a daily 10–minute strength and flexibility program in a manufacturing plant." *American Journal of Health Promotion*, 9 (1995):175–78.

Puchalski, C. M. *Official Publications of Center to Improve Care of the Dying*. The George Washington University School of Medicine, 1999. http://www.gwu.edu/~cicd/AR.HTM

Quick, J. C. "Crafting an organizational culture: herb's hand at Southwest Airlines." *Organizational Dynamics*, 21 (1992):45–56.

Quick, J. C., J. H. Gavin, C. L. Cooper and J. D. Quick. "Executive health: building strength, making risks." *Academy of Management Executive*, 14 (2000):34–46.

Quick, J. C., D. L. Nelson, J. R. Joplin and J. D. Quick. "Emotional isolation and loneliness: executive problems." *The 1992 Annual: Developing Human Resources*. Pfeiffer & Company, 1992.

Quick, J. C., D. L. Nelson, and J. D. Quick. "Successful executives: how independent?" *Academy of Management Executive*, 1 (1987):139–46.

Quick, J. C., D. L. Nelson, and J. D. Quick. *Stress and Challenge at the Top: The Paradox of the Successful Executive*. Chichester: John Wiley & Sons, 1990.

Quick, J. D., C. L. Cooper, J. H. Gavin and J. C. Quick. "Executive health: building self-reliance for challenging times." *International Review of Industrial and Organizational Psychology*, 14 (2002):187–216.

Quick, J. C., Quick, J. D. and J. H. Gavin. "Stress: measurement." In N. Schneiderman (ed.), Health Psychology Section, *Encyclopedia of Psychology*. Washington, DC: APA and Oxford University Press, USA, 2000:484–87.

Quick, J. C., Nelson, D. L., and J. J. Hurrell Jr. *Preventive Stress Management in Organizations*. Washington, DC: American Psychological Association, 1997.

Quick, J. F. "Time to Move On?" In J. C. Quick, R. Hess, J. Hermaline, and J. D. Quick, eds. *Career Stress in Changing Times*. New York: Haworth, 1990:239–50.

Rejeski, W. J., A. Thompson, P. H. Brubaker and H. S. Miller. "Acute exercise: buffering psychosocial stress responses in women." *Health Psychology*, 11 (1992): 355–62.

Rippere, V. "Nutrition and adult psychiatric problems." Paper presented at the Annual Conference, the *British Psychological Society, St Andrews*, March 1989.

Robinson, B. E. *Chained to the Desk: A Guidebook for Workaholics, Their Partners and Children, and the Clinicians Who Treat Them*. New York: New York University Press, 1998.

Roherty, J. M. *Decisions of Robert S. McNamara: A Study of the Role of the Secretary of Defense*. Coral Gables: University of Miami Press, 1970.

Romano, L. "Is Lee Iacocca a driven man? You betcha! The Chrysler Chairman, beating the odds with grit and perseverance." *The Washington Post*, September 3, 1985.

Rosch, P. J. "The quandary of job stress compensation." *Health and Stress*, 3 (2001):1–4.

Russek, H. I. and B. L. Zohman. "Relative significance of heredity, diet and occupational stress in CHD of young adults." *American Journal of Medical Sciences*, 235 (1958):266–75.

Ryff, C. D. and B. Singer. "The contours of positive human health." *Psychological Inquiry*, 9 (1998):1–28.

Salmon, P. "Emotional effects of physical exercise." In S. C. Stanford and P. Salmon (eds) *Stress: From Snyapse to Syndrome*. London: Academic Press, 1993, 395–419.

Sanchez, J. I., P. E. Spector, and C. L. Cooper. "Adapting to a boundaryless world: A developmental expatriate model." *Academy of Management Executive*, 14 (2000): 96–106.

Sanderson, S. R. and L. Schein. "Sizing up the down-sizing era." *Across the Board* 23 (1986):15–23.

Sauter, S. L., Murphy, L. R., and J. J. Hurrell. "Prevention of work-related psychological disorders: a national strategy proposed by the National Institute for Occupational Safety and Health (NIOSH)," *American Psychologist*, 45 (1990):1146–58.

Schein, E. H. "Culture: the missing concept in organization studies." *Administrative Science Quarterly*, 41 (1996): 229–40.

Schein, E. H. "Three cultures of management: the key to organizational learning." *Sloan Management Review*, 38 (1996), 9–20.

Schein, L. *Managing Culture in Mergers and Acquisitions*. New York: The Conference Board, 2001.

Schweitzer, M. E. and J. L. Kerr. "Bargaining under the influence: the role of Alcohol in Negotiations." *Academy of Management Executive*, 14 (2000):47–57.

Seligman, M. E. P. and M. Csikszentmihalyi (eds). "Positive psychology". Special issue, *American Psychologist* 55(2000).

Shaffer, M. *Life After Stress*. Chicago: Contemporary Books, 1983.

Shrivastava, P. *Bhopal: Anatomy of a Crisis*. Cambridge, MA: Ballinger, 1987.

Simmons, S. and J. C. Simmons. *Measuring Emotional Intelligence*. Arlington, TX: Summit, 1997.

Smith, A. *An Inquiry into the Nature and Causes for the Wealth of Nations*. New York: Collier, 1776.

Smith, E. T. and J. Brott. "Stress: the test Americans are failing." *Business Week*, April 18, 1988:74–77.

Snavely, J. R. *Milton S. Hershey – Builder*. Hershey, PA: Self-published, 1935.

Soames, M. *Winston and Clementine: The Personal Letters of the Churchills*. New York: Houghton Miffin, 1999.

Solomon, R. C. "Corporate roles, personal virtues: an Aristotelian approach to business ethics." *Business Ethics Quarterly*, 2 (1992):317–39.

Solomon, R. C. *Ethics and Excellence*. New York: Oxford University Press, 1992.

Solomon, R. C. *A Better Way to Think About Business*. New York: Oxford Business Press, 1999.

Spring, B., O. Maller, J. Wurtman, L. Digman and L. Cozolino. "Effects of protein and carbohydrate meals on moods and performance: interactions with sex and age." *Journal of Psychiatric Research*, 17 (1982–83): 155–67.

Stanley, T. J. and W. D. Danko. *The Millionaire Next Door: The Surprising Secrets of America's Wealthy*. Atlanta: Longstreet, 1996.

Steptoe, A., J. Moses, S. Edwards and A. Mathews. "Exercise and responsivity to mental stress: discrepancies between the subjective and physiological effects of aerobic training" (Special issue: Exercise and psychological well being. *International Journal of Sport Psychology*, 24 (1993):110–29.

Sutherland, V. and C. L. Cooper. *Strategic Stress Management: An Organizational Approach*. London: MacMillan. 1999.

Tanouye, E. "Mental illness: a rising workplace cost." *Wall Street Journal*, June 13, 2001, B1–B6.

Taylor, F. W. *Scientific Management*. New York: Harper, 1947.

Teerlink, R. and L. Ozley. *More than a Motorcycle: The Leadership Journey at Harley-Davidson*. Boston: Harvard Business School Press, 2000.

Templeton, J. M. *The Worldwide Laws of Life: 200 Eternal Spiritual Principles*. Philadelphia: Templeton Foundation, 1997.

Thomas, E. and J. Barry. "A Matter of Honor." *Newsweek*, May 27 (1996), 127 (22):24–30.

Thomas, R. D. *Dave's Way: A New Approach to Old-Fashioned Success*. New York: G. P. Putnam's Sons, 1991.

Thun, M. J., R. Peto, A. D. Lopez, *et al.* "Alcohol Consumption and Mortality among Middle-Aged and Elderly US Adults." *New England Journal of Medicine*, 337 (1997):1705–14.

Thurow, L. C. *Head to head: The Coming Economic Battle among Japan, Europe, and America*. New York: Morrow, 1992.

Tyler, C. W. Jr, and J. M. Last. "Epidemiology." In R. B. Wallace, J. M. Last, and B. N. Doebbeling, eds. *Maxcy-Rosenau-Last: Public Health and Preventive Medicine*. Stamford, CT: Appleton and Lange, 1998.

US Department of Health and Human Services. *Physical Activity and Health*. A Report of the Surgeon General. Atlanta, Georgia; US Department of Health and Human Services, Centers for Disease Control and Prevention, 1996.

US Department of Health and Human Services. *The Surgeon General's Call to Action to Prevent and Decrease Overweight and Obesity*. Rockville, MD: US Department of Health and Human Services, Public Health Service, Office of the Surgeon General, 2001 (http://www.surgeongeneral.gov/topics/obesity/).

Vaillant, G. E. *Adaptation to Life*. Boston: Little, Brown, 1977.

Veiga, J. F. "AME's Executive Advisory Panel Goes for a Check-Up." *Academy of Management Executive*, 14 (2000):25–27.

Vital Statistics of the United States, 1985, Life tables, Vol. II, Section 6. (DHHS Publication No. PHS 88–1104. January 1988). Washington DC: US Department of Health and Human Services, Public Health Service, National Center for Health Statistics, 1988.

Wall, J. F., ed. *The Andrew Carnegie Reader*. Pittsburgh: University of Pittsburgh Press, 1992.

Wall Street Journal (1982) "Disney's Epcot Center, Big $1 Billion Gamble Opens in Florida Oct. 1." September 16, 1, 21.

Wallace, R. B., J. M. Last and B. N. Doebbeling, eds. *Maxcy-Rosenau-Last: Public Health and Preventive Medicine*. Stamford, CT: Appleton and Lange, 1998.

Westman, M. "Stress and strain crossover." *Human Relations*, 54 (2001):717–49.

Westman, M., and D. Etzion, "Crossover of stress, strain and resources from one Spouse to Another." *Journal of Organizational Behavior*, 16 (1995):169–81.

Whalen, R. J. *The Founding Father: The Story of Joseph P. Kennedy*. New York: New American Library, 1964.

Wheeler, G. *Pierpont Morgan and Friends: The Anatomy of a Myth*. Prentice-Hall, Inc., Englewood Cliffs, NJ. 1967.

Wielgosz, A. T., and R. P. Nolan, "Biobehavioural Factors in the Context of Ischemic Cardiovascular Diseases." *Journal of Psychosomatic Research*, Apr–May, 48 (2000):339–45.

Williams, R. *Anger Kills*. New York: Times Books, 1993.

Williams, R., J. Kiecolt-Glazer, M. J. Legato, D. Ornish, L. H. Powell, S. L. Syme and V. Williams. "The Impact of Emotions on Cardiovascular Health." *The Journal of Gender-Specific Medicine*, 2 (1999):52–58.

Wolf, S. *Psychosocial Forces in Myocardial Infarction and Sudden Death*. In *Society, Stress and Disease*, Vol. 1 (ed L. Levi). New York: Oxford University Press, 1971.

Wolff, H. *Stress and Disease*. Springfield, IL: Charles C Thomas, 1953.

Wood, D., G. DeBacker, O. Faergeman, *et al.* "Task force report: prevention of coronary heart disease in clinical practice." *European Heart Journal*, 19 (1998):1434–1503.

Worrell, D. L., W. N. Davidson P. R. Chandy, , and S. L. Garrison. "Management turnover through deaths of key executives: effects on investor wealth." *Academy of Management Journal*, 29 (1986), 674–94.

Worrall, L. and C. L. Cooper. *Quality of Working Life Survey*. London: Institute of Management. 2001.

Wren, D. A. *Management Innovations: The People and Ideas That Have Shaped Modern Business*. New York: Oxford University Press, 1998.

Yerkes, R. M. and J. D. Dodson. "The relation of strength of stimulus to rapidity of habit-formation." *Journal of Comparative Neurology and Psychology*, 18 (1908):459–82.

Young, H. *The Iron Lady: A Biography of Margaret Thatcher*. New York: Farrar Straus Giroux, 1989.

Zaleznik, A. "The leadership gap." *Academy of Management Executive*, 4 (1990):7–22.

Ziegler, P., ed. *The Diaries of Admiral the Lord Louis Mountbatten* (two volumes). London: Collins, 1987, 1988.

Ziegler, P. *Mountbatten*. Pompano Beach, FL: Phoenix Press, 2001.

Index